Father Wasson's Story of Hope for Children

YOU ARE MY BROTHER

Photographs by Ursula Bernath • *Text by Elsbeth Day Campbell*

Our Sunday Visitor, Inc.
Noll Plaza • Huntington, IN 46750

ISBN: 0-87973-860-x
Library of Congress Catalog Card Number: 75-25340

Cover Design by James E. McIlrath

Published, printed and bound in the U.S.A. by
Our Sunday Visitor, Inc.
Noll Plaza
Huntington, Indiana 46750

860

INSIDE . . .

The story in words .... Section 1
The story in pictures .... Section 2

FOREWORD

This is a true story. Told in words and pictures it has been put together over the course of the past twenty years during which we have known Father William B. Wasson and the children he calls "Our Little Brothers and Sisters."

Photographically it is a kind of family album. It may have missed a few important scenes but hopefully not too many.

Verbally, it is impossible to put this whole story into any one book because there are too many people involved.

In addition to more than 1,000 *Pequeños* (little ones), we lack the space to mention the names of all their friends — volunteer workers and benefactors — without whose help this story could never have happened.

Ursula Bernath
Elsbeth Day Campbell

INTRODUCTION

The title of this book, *You Are My Brother,* is well chosen because based on my long acquaintance with Father Wasson and his work with orphan children, I believe it expresses a basic truth about Nuestros Pequeños Hermanos.

At the outset you might say of these children that they have three strikes against them: they are orphans; their background is one of extreme poverty and broken homes; and they live in an institution. I would say that was enough to make very maladjusted children out of them.

But, with rare exceptions, this is not so. The children at Nuestros Pequeños Hermanos are responsible; they are happy; and they feel as secure and loved as those children who live in the best of family constellations.

Now this is something most remarkable.

I believe there are few places where this could have happened. I personally do not know of one. That is why Nuestros Pequeños Hermanos has impressed me tremendously. Something has happened here which is against all prognosis, all expectations of those who deal psychologically or sociologically with these types of children.

Now, the question is: Why does it happen? What are the conditions which make it possible?

In the first place, there is one basic condition — the sense of absolute security — which every child at Nuestros Pequeños Hermanos has, namely, that he will not be dismissed for any reason whatsoever. This principle is really the principle of unconditional, motherly love. A mother loves her child unconditionally. If mothers loved their children only because they performed well or they did what the mothers liked, most infants would die.

Now this principle finds its other pole in the second principle, that of refusal to identify unconditional love with pampering which destroys the sense of responsibility and self-reliance in children. There is an atmosphere of realism, an atmosphere of expecting that they contribute, that they are responsible, that they do not indulge themselves in laziness or in passiveness, that they do something to help the community in which they live and to help it in an active and responsible way. These children are taught not only in terms of ABC's but they are taught to participate increasingly and responsibly in the social life of the community.

I would say that this could be called the fatherly principle. The motherly principle says: *I love you whatever you do.* The fatherly principle says: *I expect you to make an effort to be responsible.*

In all very healthy groups and societies, the motherly and fatherly principles (that is to say, the principles of compassion and justice) are combined. When the two principles are not combined — when they are torn apart — then both deteriorate. Compassion without the fatherly principle — without structure or justice — is an indulgence which prevents the development of the child. And justice without compassion eventually becomes cruelty and an authoritarian system in which human feelings are completely subordinated to the idea of order, work, performance. But when these two principles are combined as they are at NPH (Nuestros Pequeños Hermanos), then compassion is never passive and sentimental, and justice is never inhuman or strict.

The third principle, and one which I think is very important, is the principle of self-management. Self-management really means that people are not simply objects. It means, just to cite one example, that at Father Wasson's home the older boys take care of their kitchen. They buy food, they make the menu, they cook, they rotate assignments — and all with a minimum of supervision.

The fourth principle is stimulation. At NPH the children get courses in the native Mexican dances, in music, in singing, in art — in many things which the average child, and not only those in this low economic class but in the middle class also, is deprived of. Theirs is not merely a life of work and order but a life in which the richness of culture and stimulation is present and to which they react.

In my view it is these four principles — the principle of absolute security and at the same time of realistic responsibility; of self-management; and of stimulation — which have made it possible for this rather miraculous thing to happen at NPH.

I want to add a word about the possibility of change. So often we in the Western world think if you change one bad factor or symptom which is the cause of certain evils, then you correct the evil. The fact is, if you change one symptom you usually change nothing because you deal in all social affairs with a system and this system is very closely knit. No factor in this system can change without other factors being changed.

Let me give you a very simple example: If you want to improve slums you tear down the old houses and build new ones. This will help. But if you only do that the new houses will again become slums in a few years. You would do better to tear down and replace the worst

7

houses and spend the rest of the money for education, preparation for skilled work, health and cultural stimulation. In this way you would be trying to change the whole system rather than a single aspect of it. (Of course, a slum neighborhood is only a subrogation within the larger system of society. Without changing the whole system, not too much can be done for the small system.)

You see the same thing in individuals. If you try to change one symptom, then usually a person may suppress or repress that particular symptom, but it will come up somewhere else. You can really change symptoms only if you change the psychical structure as a whole, and create a new structure. This is precisely what I think has happened at NPH. With all of the principles I have mentioned, an entirely new structure has been created. None of them alone could have made this achievement possible.

I want to make it very clear that the important point here is that Father Wasson has not tried to change one factor but that he has brought together a number of principles which, in their conjunction, make it possible for this family of more than 1,000 children to react as it does.

Finally, I want to say a word about Father Wasson. What has happened at NPH is only possible because he lives the principles which are expressed in his work. In other words, he is credible. Youngsters are suspicious and particularly those whose life experience is one of being deceived or brutally treated. It is quite clear that with all of these principles the system could not have succeeded at NPH unless the children could believe in the principles because they saw their manifestation in Father Wasson.

I do not mean to imply that NPH is a unique experiment which could not exist elsewhere. I think if the system which is applied at NPH were studied, then there might be other Father Wassons who could undertake the same kind of work he is doing which today they lack the courage to do because everyone says it is impossible. But one point must be clear: such work can be done only by people who do not work "bureaucratically." Father Wasson is a loving man, a man of extraordinary talent for organizing, a man of great concentration — but he is no bureaucrat. If he were, his work would not be what it is.

What he has shown is that one can organize and be efficient without bureaucratic spirit but with the spirit of humanism and reason. This was not rare in the distant past and perhaps it will become frequent again in the future. Father Wasson has demonstrated that it is possible. Those who believe in the non-bureaucratic way of human organization can learn a lot from his work; those who don't will not be able to imitate it.

Dr. Erich Fromm

8

ONE

When the first light of dawn comes to Cuernavaca the clouds begin to lift. Carried by the breeze, they climb to the top of the mountains leaving the valley wide open to the arrival of the sun. . . .

At that moment, however, the new day had not yet come, the night was dark. It had stopped raining but water was still running down the gutters of the narrow, slanting streets where houses and shops seemed to huddle around the old market. Overlooking it stood the little church of Tepetates, its two tall cedar trees like guardians in its tiny gate-enclosed front patio.

Down below, among the hooded market stalls that smelled of yesterday's fruit, a boy was moving stealthily. Surefooted as a cat and with the ease of practice he darted from one group of shadows to the next, zigzagging as he approached the church on the side where its patio wall was lowest.

He was thinking bitterly that he knew the streets of Cuernavaca better at night than in the daytime. During the day he could pretend that nothing had changed, that his father was still alive; but at night his stepfather would return to the house — impossible now to think of it as home — and the angry scenes would begin again.

The man would start to complain that he had married the mother of a street rat, a thief and worse. If his mother tried to stand up for him, the man would go for her. If he were drunk which he very often was, he would beat her. Her screams made the boy feel powerless — he was only a boy, the man big and powerful. Actually it had been a relief when his stepfather had ended by throwing him out of the house. That last night, however, his mother had not spoken up for him. She had let him go.

So now, he thought as he reached the wall, he was free. He was alone. He could do what he pleased. Nobody cared.

He put his hands on top of the wall, and looked over it. There was no light, no sound.

Tossing his head so as to jerk his stringy hair out of his face, he jumped and landed on his feet. Quickly he crossed the patio and taking a bunch of keys out of his pocket, he opened the door of the sacristy.

He even smiled as he remembered how angry Agustín, the sacristan, had been when he discovered

9

the loss of his keys. Served him right. Too stingy to have duplicate sets made, Agustín had to leave them on a hook in the open corridor for the use of everybody who needed them — his wife and the nuns who tended the dispensary.

The dispensary had been recently installed by the new priest, a tall thin American whose name was Father Wasson. He spoke Spanish with difficulty, mispronouncing words and sometimes using the wrong ones but there was no question that he was very eager to help people, especially children. It was for them that he had installed the medical dispensary and the kitchen where food was given to the hungry. The fact that there were always so many children milling about had made it very easy to steal the keys. Agustín had expostulated angrily when he discovered they were gone. He had shouted, waved his arms and shooed all the kids down the front stairs into the street below.

That had been days ago the boy went on to think. Tonight he had shut himself into the sacristy. He had to hurry, do what he had come to do and get out. He started to panic but then forced himself to keep calm, to wait until his eyes got used to the darkness. He did not need to turn on the light. He knew the place well, as did the other boys who had been acolytes. The other boys would not dare do what he was doing tonight.

He knew exactly where the desk was. He went to it, opened the draw-er. He started to take money out of envelopes. He knew what they were — the donations that Father Wasson was collecting to paint the church.

The boy froze. He heard sounds — voices, footsteps, a police whistle! Quickly he stuffed the money into his pockets, ran to the door of the sacristy and out into the patio. Too late! There were policemen everywhere! He crouched low in a corner.

Agustín, the sacristan, tells the story this way:

"I had been expecting something like this to happen. Ever since I'd lost my keys, I had stayed awake every night. Father Wasson had told me not to worry. He told me to pray for the thief and leave it in God's hands. I prayed and stayed awake. Sure enough, well past midnight I heard a scratching noise. At first I thought it was cats. Then I saw the boy jump over the wall.

"He looked almost as big as a man. I thought, 'What shall I do?' Our window overlooked the patio of the house next door which at that time belonged to Don Wulfrano.

"As fast as I could I jumped out the window calling in loud whispers: 'Don Wulfrano, Don Wulfrano, please let me in. I must call the police. The church is being robbed!' "

The police arrived very quickly. They found the boy crouched low in the corner of the corridor behind some buckets with tall stemmed flowers in them.

"It is a serious matter, Padre,"

10

Agustín reported to Father Wasson the following morning. "I often wonder if it is wise to let these no-good boys hang around here. You allow them to be acolytes and now look what's happened. I figure there is a loss of about 500 pesos. I hope you can get it back."

"Did you recognize the boy?" Father Wasson asked.

"I've seen him before. He seems to be about 15 years old. I think his name is Carlos, but I'm not sure. There are so many of them because you are always kind to them, Padre."

The priest took a deep breath. "Agustín," he said, "I want you to pray for him. I will go now to see if the police will let us have him."

"Let us have him? Do you mean, you would ask for custody of him?" Agustín was aghast. "Padre, you can't do that. You would be responsible for him, or we would! What are we going to do with him? We can't put him here."

Father Wasson was halfway down the stairs of the church. Turning, he said, "We must help him, Agustín. He is our brother."

It was unusual for the Mass in English to start late on Sunday. Held at the church of the Franciscan Third Order (the one just inside the cathedral grounds), it always began promptly at 9:30 a.m. but that Sunday five minutes passed, ten, a quarter of an hour. The well-dressed members of the congregation, most of them Americans, were alternately looking at their watches and at one another.

They began to talk in loud whispers. Was there going to be Mass? Perhaps they had better go to another church. It was almost 10 o'clock. Walter Nolan, a retired Mexican-born Irishman, offered to go to the cathedral cloister to make inquiries, but his wife said: "No, wait. Here comes the bishop."

Everyone turned and watched respectfully as Bishop Sergio Méndez Arceo came in the side door from the cathedral courtyard. Tall, broad-shouldered, wearing his purple cassock and red skull cap, he strode up the aisle.

Turning to face the congregation, he said, "My friends, forgive me for keeping you waiting. I will be brief. Two years ago when I was appointed to this diocese I realized what an attraction Cuernavaca, our city of eternal springtime, has for people of other countries, particularly the United States. Persons like you come here for extended vacations or decide to stay here after you retire. I have been trying for some time to provide a priest for you who speaks English. Today I have brought him to you. Permit me to introduce him: Father William Wasson."

Virginia Nolan said later: "I looked at Bill Wasson that day. He stepped out of the sacristy all of a sudden. He looked young, eager, but so thin and pale. I told my husband:

11

'He'll never last!' Walter said he looked as though he might be lonely and that we should ask him to our house. So we did.''

This was going to develop into a lifelong friendship, in spite of the fact that at first Father Bill Wasson tried to refuse the Nolans' invitation. He told them he did not want to become involved in social obligations because he had so many other ones. He was still in charge of the Tepetates church. He told Virginia Nolan about the dispensary he had set up so that medicines and food could be provided for the people of the market and their children. Mrs. Nolan offered to help and she did.

From then on, the Nolans welcomed his frequent visits to their home. He told them about his problems, his hopes, his dreams.

He told them how he had happened to come to Mexico. Born in Phoenix, Arizona, he had studied for the priesthood at a Benedictine college in Missouri but a few months before his ordination, he had been denied it on the grounds of bad health. The doctors diagnosed his case as a progressive thyroid deficiency which, they gloomily foretold, would incapacitate him. Undaunted he recovered, took a Master's degree in Law and Social Sciences and then worked for a time in the placement and rehabilitation of juvenile delinquents in Phoenix.

As a boy he had helped his father do that kind of work. His parents, William J. and Mary Was-son, spent their lives, their time and their money helping less fortunate people. The things he did as a child in the effort to follow their example sometimes made his mother laugh. She recalls that at the age of 10 he would bring stray dogs home because, he claimed, they were lonely, uncared for and had no place to go.

At the age of 15 he had permission from the juvenile-court judge in Phoenix to take detained boys to his parents' home for the weekend. In getting to know them, he had become convinced that their situation could have been prevented in most cases.

"There is no such thing as a bad child," he explained to the Nolans in one of his first long chats at their home. "He may behave badly because he feels abandoned and alone.

"There is nothing so tragic as a lonely child. A child having parents has care, love, interest, prayers, attention in sickness and a solution to his problems and troubles. Take a 12-year-old boy with no parents or friends. If he is truly alone, to whom can he turn, what can he do? His first impulse will lead him to steal food for survival. He is like a dry leaf fallen from a tree and blown about by the wind."

That early contact with juvenile delinquents had seeded the idea of the priesthood in Bill Wasson's mind so that he could minister to unwanted or abandoned children whose loneliness could be supplanted with love in the security of a home. There

12

they could recover that trust which circumstances beyond their control had killed in their hearts and minds. However, all that was not clear in Bill Wasson's own mind when he first thought of it. In the beginning it was more of a vague longing, a dream which he began to lose hope of ever realizing because every time he tried to work, his health broke down and for that reason no bishop in the United States would risk ordaining him.

Almost as a last resort, hoping the change of climate would help him, he came to Mexico in 1949. Here he found a doctor who, not promising a complete cure, did alleviate his condition. For a time he became a university professor and student counselor in Mexico City. Then a friend recommended him to Bishop Méndez Arceo who ordained him on Pentecost Sunday in 1953.

"From the very beginning, he had the bishop's permission to found a home for poor children in Cuernavaca," recalls Mrs. Nolan, "and even before he took in his first boy (the thief of Tepetates church) he kept asking me to find a suitable house for that purpose. I remember the day he was at our house on Calle Alvaro Obregón, he was pacing up and down our living room, saying he had to get started. It was his vocation, the reason he had been ordained," Mrs. Nolan recalls him saying. "He kept begging me to help him find a building where he could lodge children. He didn't have any

yet, not even his first boy, yet he knew what kind of a place he wanted. It would have to be roomy, he said, have plumbing facilities and be inexpensive. He had no money for his project; neither had we and he knew the bishop was not able to help him financially. Maybe, he suggested, I could find somebody who would give us a house."

She told him that finding a suitable place sounded difficult enough. She had visions of having to search high and low, all over Cuernavaca for it. However, the very next day she saw there was a "For Rent" sign on a big ramshackle building almost next door to her own house on Obregón.

The building was or had been a warehouse. The people of the neighborhood called it the *cervecería* (brewery or alehouse). It had at one time been used as a beer storage and distribution center. A new owner used it as a lumberyard until he died; then his family decided to rent it.

Virginia Nolan phoned Father Wasson to let him know about it. Father went to see it with another friend, Hans Mattes, a German businessman who was a member of the Third Order church congregation and an acquaintance of the recently deceased owner.

Things were at this stage when the boy who robbed the Tepetates church was caught. When Mattes learned that Father had obtained custody of this boy, he offered to pay

13

the first month's rent on the empty warehouse immediately.

"Come on, Father, let's take it," Mattes urged. "You haven't got room in your apartment for three people — you, the boy and Leonardo."

Leonardo was Father Wasson's helper. He ran errands, did the cooking and cleaning. His tasks also included accompanying the priest on his visits to people in jail as well as hospitals.

"The building," Mattes was saying that day, "needs fixing up. It lacks so many things. I have talked to my wife. Father, are you listening to me?" demanded Mattes who recognized the 1,000-yard stare on the priest's face and knew his thoughts were on future uses and not present limitations of the building.

"My wife and I are about to celebrate our 25th wedding anniversary. We are going on a trip but we've decided that if you want that building for a home for poor children, we will give you the money to pay the first month's rent and perhaps fix it up a little."

Mattes and his wife, as Father Wasson knew, had no children of their own. They were offering something as a sacrifice to themselves in a way that he could not refuse. Yet what really forced him to make a decision was a telephone call.

It was the Chief of Police saying he had eight more boys. Did Father want them?

"We moved in the same day," Leonardo remembers. "Such a large empty building! It had no kitchen, no furniture. We had no beds, no chairs, no table, no pots, no pans, no blankets, no towels. Do you know what it is to have nothing? But we were happy because we had a father who loved us.

"You see," Leonardo explained many years later, "I met Father Wasson back in 1952 before he was ordained. I was 18 years old at the time and worked at the hotel where he used to stay when he first started to come to Cuernavaca. One day he asked me why I was so sad. I told him my father had died. He asked me if I would like to go with him and be his assistant. He couldn't pay me, he said, but he'd see to it that I lacked nothing. To me it was like finding a new father.

"So when the police let us have the first boy and then the other eight, I felt they were my younger brothers.

"I looked after them and they helped me. We moved into the building and cleaned it up as much as we possibly could. We found a lot of wood and an old door which we scrubbed and set up on sawhorses to serve as a makeshift table. With the wood we built a fire in the patio. I borrowed a cooking pot from Mrs. Nolan. I don't know what I would have done without her in those early days; she was my right arm.

"When Father saw that I was cooking some beans and had sent for tortillas he decided to celebrate by

14

inviting Mr. and Mrs. Nolan to supper."

It must have been a strange scene, almost unreal. The tall blond young priest, nine boys — street urchins and ragamuffins — staring wide-eyed with astonishment at finding themselves sitting on empty crates around the makeshift table in an enormous but otherwise empty house.

"I remember," Virginia Nolan was to say later, "that Leonardo managed to serve the beans and tortillas on the lid of the pot I'd lent him. He had not asked me for either plates or forks. We ate the beans with the tortillas. We talked and we laughed. Walter said to Father, 'Well, you've founded it,' but Father looked at the boys and at us. 'We've founded it,' he said softly and then exultantly: 'We've founded it! We've founded it!' "

But when his guests had gone home, Father Wasson stood motionless for a long time in the semidarkness of the large hall where the intermittent lights of the passing traffic lighted up the walls and corners, revealing the small mounds of boys who lay huddled together on the bare floor. How many times had he seen children sleeping like that on the streets, boys huddled on doorsteps, covered with rags and old newspapers to keep themselves warm? Had he improved their condition by bringing them here?

This house was so big, would he ever be able to fill it, make it warm, comfortable, give it a feeling of home?

He began to pray. The traffic passing along the street outside threw spurts of light through the curtainless windows.

It was the 2nd of August, 1954.

TWO

At first there were nine boys, then came another three. "The perfect number," said Father, "like the twelve Apostles."

But word spread fast and people came bringing more children; a family of seven brothers, the youngest aged 7; another family of ten orphans: boys and girls and a 6-month-old baby. Father Wasson explained that he had no one to help him take care of girls or babies, he could only accept boys. Soon he had twenty-four.

People brought them gifts — a kitchen stove, beds and blankets, clothes, odd pieces of furniture, old tattered comics, three white goats (a nanny and her kids), and a dog (partly dachshund).

There are many stories about this first dog. One is that he was given the name of Stonewall Jackson because he preferred stone walls to trees. The boys remember that there was a man who used to pass the house every day selling doughnuts. None of them ever had any money so one day they offered to trade their dog for twenty-four doughnuts, one for each of them. The man agreed and Jackson obediently trotted off with him. Two days later Jackson came home. An-

other legend is that the dog got run over by a car and was so badly mangled that everyone was sure he would die; but he didn't. Although one of his hind legs was never quite right and after that he limped, he lived for such a long time and the boys became so fond of him that when he finally died, they insisted on having him stuffed. Father Wasson who cannot resist puns once commented that Jackson ended by having more stuffing in him dead than alive.

In those early days the boys hardly ever had enough to eat. It is only logical to suppose that if their dog ate, it was because they shared their food with him.

Fortunately, people quite often brought gifts of food, particularly the merchants of the Tepetates market. They'd ring the doorbell and disappear.

At the doorstep there would be a sack of beans, a crate of tomatoes or a bag of rice.

One day an old woman, driving a flock of turkeys, knocked at the door asking for Padre Wasson. No, he wasn't in; would she mind waiting for him? No, she said, she had to get to the market to sell her turkeys and, Christmas being near at hand,

16

consisted exclusively of donations. In order to obtain these he has always had to spend a good deal of his time with friends who in turn put him in touch with their acquaintances and friends. Sometimes they brought whole groups to visit him and his children.

Quite early one morning a delegation of Mexican women arrived unannounced at the former warehouse on Obregón Street. Father nearly had a fit. The boys had not yet swept the hall nor finished cleaning the dormitory. The *basura* man (trash collector) had not come by. There was an evil-smelling stack of uncovered trash cans out back.

Boys came and went, talking their heads off. Glaring at them, Father scratched his ear and wished desperately that his mother or Virginia Nolan were there to help him show those guests around.

Suddenly aware that they had a leader and that she was asking him questions, he pulled himself together.

How many boys did he have? What were their ages? What did he feed them? What did he do if they got sick? How did he manage to clothe them? Who were they? Where did they come from? What were his requisites for receiving them?

"And what," asked the spokeswoman, "are you going to call them, Father?"

"Call them?"

"They should have a name, don't you think?" She looked at him, her eyes softening. "How do you feel towards them?"

"They are our little brothers," he said.

"Nuestros pequeños hermanos," she repeated in Spanish. "It's in the Bible somewhere, isn't it? Oh, I remember! Whatever you do unto these the smallest of my brothers, you do unto me. Is that right, Father?"

He smiled. *"Estos mis hermanos más pequeños.* My Spanish is improving," he said.

When the women had gone he looked it up in the Bible. It was in Matthew, chapter 25, verses 35-40.

In January, 1955, a new boy arrived. He was called José Bahena but he had to change his first name to Lauro. Years later he explained why: "When I arrived at Nuestros Pequeños Hermanos there was already another José. Father Wasson thought it would be too confusing to have two Josés and as I had been the second to arrive I had to change my name.

"We lived in Taxco. My mother died soon after I was born and my father, seven years later. I had two older sisters; one got married and the other one wanted to be a nun. Not knowing what to do with me, she took me with her to the convent. I lived with the Sisters for a short time, but there was a German priest who knew Father Wasson, so it was arranged that I come to Cuernavaca.

19

"I remember when I arrived that there were twenty-six of us and we kept chickens."

Friends kept suggesting to Father Wasson that he make his boys self-supporting. In an effort to help him do this, one benefactor presented him with 150 laying hens, so the boys could run an egg and poultry business. About this time, two enthusiastic gentlemen arrived from the United States to teach the boys how to make candy and cookies to sell. Both projects ended in failure. The nature of the merchandise proved too much of a temptation to growing youngsters whose normal diet consisted of beans, rice and tortillas. Deliveries of cookies and candy became mysteriously lost en route. The chickens developed a strange disease which began to kill them off one at a time but the strange thing was they disappeared, feathers and all. The boys said an animal called a *tlacoache* was eating them or maybe it was a coyote. One night, however, Father Wasson woke up and sniffed: a delicious odor was coming from the back patio, of chicken being roasted on a spit.

Although he walloped the culprits lustily with an oversized *huarache* and promptly sold the rest of the chickens, the failure of the would-be commercial enterprises did not disturb him. What weighed heavily on his mind and spirit was the education of his children. Public schools were both un-

derstaffed and overpopulated. He could not afford a private school. What he really wanted was to start his own school.

This seemed completely impossible until one day a soft-spoken Mexican gentleman knocked at the door, introduced himself as a teacher and offered his services free of charge. He began teaching the first three grades of elementary school to the *Pequeños* in their home and later, thanks to the generosity of the owner and director, the *Pequeños* were able to attend fourth, fifth and sixth grades at the English school in Cuernavaca. The boys studied and received the certified paper which the Federal System of Education requires of each pupil who finishes six years in the elementary grades.

Late one rainy afternoon in June, 1955, Agustín, the sacristan of the Tepetates church, was trudging along the narrow sidewalk of Obregón Street trying to cover two little boys and himself with his umbrella. What hampered his movements was the fact that both boys, who were pale and frightened, and shivering with cold, clung for dear life to his free hand and stayed so close that it was difficult for him to walk.

Shepherding them along as best he could, he wondered whether their tears were real or they were raindrops trickling down their upturned faces. He himself felt badly shaken by the scene they had just witnessed: the mother's agony, the doc-

20

tor's helpless shrug as he said, "She is dying." Those dark, wide-open eyes in the boys' drawn faces reflected pools of fear and anguish.

Agustín now upbraided himself for not having gone sooner to fetch the children from the hospital. Father Wasson had asked him as a special favor to keep in touch with the case. Father was no longer at the church of Tepetates. The bishop had relieved him of his duties there. His *Pequeños* required more attention and he still had to officiate at the church of the Third Order. In spite of this, however, Agustín kept in close touch with him.

"I want you to do me a special favor, Agustín," Father Wasson had said. "There is a poor woman in the *hospital civil*. She has an incurable disease. I have promised her that when she dies, I will take care of her two sons. Will you bring them to me when the time comes?"

When the time comes! Agustín fumed at himself, pushing the umbrella forward over the two boys and feeling the rain trickle down the back of his neck. Had he had to wait for the moment when the mother had been actually dying? Why, in God's name, couldn't he have fetched those boys sooner?

"Gracias a Dios," Agustín gasped aloud, "we have arrived. Will you let go of my hand, boys, so I can knock at the door? You are going to be all right now." Glory be, he thought, for suddenly to his astonishment they beamed happily at

him. Why, he thought, we haven't even gone in, they haven't even seen Father and they already look happy, as though they hear something they recognize. Well, what is it?

The door opened to the sound of music. Inside the boys were singing and in their midst was Father Wasson leading the melody on his accordion. He stopped, came forward, arms stretched wide enough to engulf Agustín in an embrace that seemed to grow, for it both widened and moved downward to include the two small newcomers who, not quite knowing how it had happened, found themselves transferred from the man who had brought them to the man who now faced them with an affectionate smile.

"Would you like to come into my office?" Father asked the two boys. Their dazed expressions were the only response as they looked up at him. "You see, when boys like you come here for the first time, we have a talk so that we can come to a decision on whether you want to stay and join our family because that is what it is — a family."

Father Wasson did not ask Agustín into his office, only the two boys. After he had closed the door and they were alone he sat down at his desk and said: "My name is Father Wasson. Perhaps Agustín or your mother told you about me."

The older boy nodded while the other's wide black eyes seemed fixed on the priest as if trusting his whole being to him.

"What are your names?"

"Cirilo and Memo Mejía at your service, Padre," the elder of the two answered in one spurt as he snapped to attention like a soldier.

"Son, would you like to tell me what happened?" He tried to create a warm feeling, stretching out his hands, and drawing the boys closer, gently, silently.

Cirilo nodded again. Tight-lipped, molding his words he began: "That morning I was trying to look after Memo, my brother, and keep the beans and coffee warm. My father had gone out. I knew he would fly into a rage as he always did if he came home and the food was not warm. He had gone to see my mother in prison. She was there because of him. He had been caught with marijuana. When he was first imprisoned, my mother went to see him and he persuaded her to smuggle him in some. She was frightened but she was more afraid of not doing what he said. She hid the marijuana carefully, but they caught her and put her in jail, too. For a time my brother and I lived with her in prison but when my father was released first, he took us out with him."

Cirilo paused. For the first time he relaxed. "My father was a musician," he said. "He played the guitar. At family fiestas he always sang; his beautiful voice seemed the most marvelous thing about him and it made us feel music was so natural, so easy, so wonderful." He paused again as though to catch on to his memory. "That morning I was fanning the charcoal fire when the neighbors ran to tell us. A bus was speeding down the street. My father saw a woman start to cross. He threw himself at her and hurled her to safety, but he was run over and killed. He died instantly, they said."

"He saved a life."

"Yes, he saved a life but it was not my mother's. She came back to us, but she was sick with that terrible pain and now she is dead, too." Cirilo's voice stopped. Chin up, he was staring at nothing with dull, unfocused eyes.

Father Wasson took off his glasses and wiped them with a handkerchief. He cleared his throat, turned his chair sideways, beckoned to the two boys and put an arm around each of them.

Memo, the younger of the brothers, looked up at him asking: "We are going to stay, ¿verdad?"

"Yes, it is true," answered Father Bill Wasson, "this is your home now."

Memo explained later: "If I say that from that moment on we thought of him as our father, I do not mean that he became a substitute. He is the kind of father all of us would like to have. Some of us had lacked certain things; he gave them to us. I don't mean material things although I never will forget the day he asked me how much a guitar cost. That wasn't until years later after I had studied and obtained

22

good grades at school. I told him about 300 pesos. He gave me the money and told me to buy myself a guitar. I was delighted but it was more than the guitar — he did things for us that changed our lives. They banished our fears, made it possible for us to hope. I shall never stop being grateful to him," Memo said many years later.

THREE

It was the autumn of 1955. Among the often odd assortment of gifts that the benefactors sent the *Pequeños*, there was a battered old radio which they liked to play as loud as possible. When Father Wasson was in, he always asked them to tune it down or turn it off but that afternoon he was out. The music blared when it was suddenly interrupted by a news bulletin.

Cyclone "Hilda" had struck the port of Tampico. The announcer went from one fact to the next: there were terrific floods, thousands of people left homeless, hundreds of children roaming the street, their parents lost or dead.

When Father Wasson came home that evening, he was not surprised to find the boys waiting for him just inside the front door. They always did, usually pouncing on him the minute he appeared; the smallest ones scrambling over each other like puppies, each wanting to be hugged; all of them trying to talk at the same time. But that evening even the little boys looked solemn and none of them spoke.

"Is anything wrong?" Father asked anxiously, beginning to count the boys.

"Nothing has happened to us, Padre," one who had obviously been appointed spokesman replied. "We have been listening to the radio, hearing about the terrible flood in Tampico. The radio said there are hundreds of children there who have lost their homes and their parents. We have been talking it over and we think that you should go there and bring some of those children here."

"Do you mean, here, to our house?" He had no money to go to Tampico, hardly enough to cover expenses. He told them so, but either they didn't believe him or they were convinced that he was capable of anything.

"Supposing," he probed, "that I find a way to do what you suggest, would you be willing to share your beds, your food with the boys from Tampico? Would you be willing to sleep on the floor and eat very much less than you do now in order to help those who have been left without a home? The decision is yours to make. You do not have to make it tonight. Think it over and tell me in the morning."

"Whatever we can, we will do, but you must go to Tampico," was the straightforward answer the boys gave him the following day.

Father went off to Mexicana

24

Airlines where officials gave him a free ticket on a commercial flight and promised to put a cargo plane at his disposal for his return trip.

"It was the worst disaster that had ever struck Tampico," remembers Rodolfo González who twenty years later was to become Father Wasson's assistant and general administrator of Nuestros Pequeños Hermanos. "We lived downtown. The streets were rivers rushing into whirlpools at every corner. Some people had managed to take refuge in the sturdiest buildings of the city. Others were less fortunate. I saw families that were separated, some members on one side of the torrent, the others on the opposite side. Men in all types of boats, including canoes, were trying to haul people across, but the debris dragged at the boats, obstructing and capsizing them."

The greatest losses, Father Wasson learned, had been suffered by people living on the outskirts of the city. In the low-lying area where the river, the lagoon and the swamp converged were the ramshackle wooden huts of the poor. Only a few standing on higher ground had escaped being swept away.

On that first trip to Tampico Father Wasson looked not only for orphans but for the children of the families in direst need. There was one family of eight children, three girls and five boys. The widowed mother made a living by taking in

washing, but now she and her own were homeless. Neighbors offered to help, but no one could house them all. Father offered to take two of the older boys.

"A similar thing happened to my family," Rodolfo González remembers. "On his first trip, Father took my brother and two of my cousins. I was 15 years old at the time and I really didn't want to go with them as I was already working. However, the next year Father sent for me. In fact, for several years after that he came back to Tampico to gather up those of us who were relatives of the first thirty-nine boys he took to Cuernavaca."

Those first thirty-nine were never going to forget the flight on the cargo plane. They had to tie themselves to the inside of the empty plane to avoid being tossed about. They were violently ill and scared out of their wits. However, they remember that when they landed at the Mexico City airport they were met by some very important people and taken to an impressive restaurant after which they were put in Red Cross ambulances. Sirens shrieking, before they quite knew where they were going, they headed at full speed towards Cuernavaca.

That night in the house on Obregón Street, where there had been thirty boys, there were sixty-nine. Two slept in each bed, the rest on the floor. There was only one bathroom and as often happens in Cuernavaca, there was no water

25

next morning. During the weeks that followed, the boys came down with the epidemic flu; Father ran out of funds; there was no money to pay the rent; and Jackson got run over.

Just as everything seemed to be going wrong, a Scotsman who had lived in Mexico for many years gave Father Wasson a house — a ranch-like building located on a large piece of land in Colonia Buenavista on the northern edge of Cuernavaca.

"It had plumbing facilities in working order," Father recalls. "It was our own home and we moved in just before Christmas of 1955." The move was expensive.

One afternoon when Father's funds were nil, he called the boys and asked them to pray. The doorbell rang. It was a chauffeur who had an envelope he said he must deliver personally to Father Wasson.

Inside was a check for a large amount of money and a letter: ". . . My only daughter, Kathleen, died a few days ago at the age of 5. I know you only have boys, but in addition to the enclosed, may I also send you the Christmas presents I had for her? Please pray. . . ." It was signed "Carmen."

Father realized who she was, a wealthy young woman who sometimes came to Cuernavaca on weekends. He had noticed her and her beautiful little daughter at the church of the Third Order. He was very sorry indeed to learn that the child had died, he told her chauffeur, asking him for her address so that he might call personally to thank her and offer his condolences.

José Díaz was a happy young man; he was a bachelor, a good carpenter with a job he liked in a furniture factory. He walked to work every morning and every day Father Wasson, who at that time drove the boys to the English school in his old station wagon, overtook Díaz and offered him a lift. Díaz smiled and politely refused explaining that he liked to walk. One day Father Wasson finally managed to persuade him to get into the car.

"I want you to work for me," Father said bluntly.

"Doing what, Padre?"

"Taking care of children."

"Taking care of . . .? Why I don't even think I like them. Oh well, one of these days I might marry and of course, I will want children of my own, but in the meantime, I'm perfectly satisfied just being a carpenter. Besides, I'm earning a good salary. I don't suppose you could pay me?"

"No," Father Wasson said. "I will give you room and board and a small stipend. When will you start working for me?"

"I don't want to work for you."

"I need a driver. If you don't want to look after boys, you can drive this station wagon."

"Which is always full of boys," the young man replied. "I don't want to. Why should I?"

Years later, José Díaz said, "I

couldn't have refused more bluntly. I was even rude but he would not leave me in peace. It got so bad that one time I actually hid from him. The next time he saw me he was furious, demanding to know where I had been. You would have thought he had some power over me: he did not. I had no intention of working for him but do you know what? One Sunday morning, I turned up at the place he had told me to go with my suitcase in one hand and my box of tools in the other.''

At the time Díaz arrived there were seventy-two boys and for each twelve there was one counselor. In the beginning these counselors were adults, usually volunteers, but later when the number of children increased considerably, Father Wasson began to name *Pequeños* as counselors (or commissioners, as they were later called). It is by means of this system of counseling that Father Wasson has tried to conserve the personal touch with the children even though the number of the latter has increased throughout the years.

Father tried for a time not to change the numbers which had for him a biblical significance; that of seventy-two Disciples and twelve Apostles. Nevertheless, he kept on accepting more boys. He wanted to go back to Tampico and soon found out that Díaz did have a driver's license.

''The first time I drove him to Tampico was in 1956,'' remembers Díaz. ''After that we went at least once a year. Sometimes we would take the *Pequeños* who had come from there so that they could visit their families. It became known that Father always stayed at the same hotel where people would come asking him for help. Sometimes they would be the relatives or friends of orphaned children, or the children themselves.''

One day two boys came to the hotel. They looked about 8 and 10 years old. They had a 5-year-old sister, they said. Their father had abandoned them. Their mother had to work but she was not strong and found it increasingly harder to look after them. Father Wasson visited the mother. She was young, beautiful, a foreigner. Her little daughter was 5 years old. A bell seemed to ring in his mind, reminding him of the wealthy young woman in Cuernavaca whose own 5-year-old daughter had died.

He picked up the telephone and asked for long distance. He was very brief. ''Carmen,'' he said, ''I am bringing you a little girl.'' He hung up without waiting for a reply.

It was on his next trip to Tampico that Father brought back the shoeshine boy. He tells his own story:

''My name is José Vicencio. I was born on the 23rd of December, 1949, in the happy-go-lucky port town of Tuxpan, Veracruz. As I remember, my father had no school-

27

ing and he lacked the energy to look for work. My proud mother was just the same. So what was to be my future in spite of the fact that I was their only child? I saw very clearly that I would have to fend for myself because I mattered to nobody.

"I was 6 years old when I decided to leave home without even asking for permission. A friend, whom I still remember gratefully, built a shoeshine box for me. I learned the trade very quickly and that was how I earned enough money to eat. At the age of 8 I wasn't going to school but I did know how to read and write because I figured it out. I learned by reading the signs on the shop windows, the names of the stores, magazines and the like. Then I learned how to write, how to count and add numbers.

"I never went back home and my parents didn't look for me. I lived as a vagabond, earning my own money, eating alone, sleeping by myself. My only friends were the boys on the streets. They were good to me and I liked being with them. We played and sometimes ate together. Many times I slept with them in those makeshift shacks they built with bits of cardboard and pieces of old wood on the outskirts of the city.

"One day I got them together and asked them: '*Compañeros* (companions), I want to go to Tampico. Who wants to come along with me?' They stared at me and questioned each other with their eyes.

They didn't answer. I insisted that we must change our surroundings, and soon.

" 'If we don't like it, we can come back,' I told them, 'but it has to be all or none of us.'

" 'Well,' one said, 'let's all go and whoever doesn't like it can come back, okay?'

"We agreed. We got to Tampico and all of us liked it. There we began a new life as a continuation of the one we had brought with us. We'd go to the movies together almost every day. At night, we'd just walk around the town until 1, 2, or 3 o'clock in the morning.

"One night, it was 2 a.m., the police grabbed us. Some boys ran and managed to escape. Others of us got caught. We all protested. Why should the police arrest us? We had done nothing wrong.

"The answer was that we were minors and should not have been wandering around the streets at that hour of the night. We were to be held in prison for three or even five days. There were four of us.

"The afternoon of the second day there came a man dressed in black. His skin was white. He smiled. He looked like a foreigner. He was accompanied by a man and a police officer.

"The man who was with him said: 'I want to introduce Father Wasson to you. He has a home in Cuernavaca for boys who don't have any parents, who are poor and want to study, live cleanly and eat well.

28

This is a good opportunity for anybody who wants it.'

"The priest kept looking at us and smiling.

"I began to wonder whether to let myself be convinced or whether I wanted to go on living as I was.

"The man asked the question again: 'Who wants to go? Nobody? I advise you not to let this opportunity pass. Do you want to continue being vagrants?'

"By this time we were all arguing but suddenly there was the answer. Three of us decided to go.

" 'All right,' said the priest, 'you are going to talk to this man who is with me and then we'll go.'

"I was the first one to talk to the man who, I discovered, was the priest's driver.

"I told him the story of my life, we came to an agreement and I decided to go along.

"My companions also said they would go but at the last minute they changed their minds. I almost backed out, too, but I said to myself: the step has been taken, I will go forward, not back. They bought me some clothes and that same day we left for Cuernavaca where a new phase of life began.

"It was the life of a large, noisy family of boys, none of whom I'd ever seen before, but although I was a stranger to them they behaved as though I were their brother. We had to share everything, including schoolbooks of which we never had enough. We had to share in doing all the work of the house and helping Leonardo in the kitchen.

"We made our own tortillas. When the machine broke down you should have seen the fat shapeless *gordas* (thick tortillas) we turned out.

"One of the boys, Memo, told me the same thing had happened about the bread. Leonardo had sent some of the boys to a friendly baker who had promised to teach them to make *teleras* (Mexican rolls with slashes on top). The boys did their best but they just could not manage to indent the buns in the right places. All they managed to produce were smooth round buns. Leonardo laughed and said: 'Oh well, let's call it *pan bola* (bread rolls).' We are still making it; it is a specialty of the house.

"I remember at first in Buenavista there was no dining room. We ate in the patio in the shade of the laurel tree or we'd climb it and eat perched on a branch. It was in the patio that we played ball and also heard Mass.

"There was a little chapel, so tiny that we used to joke about it, saying that when Father said, *'Dominus Vobiscum,'* he had to stretch his arms out vertically instead of horizontally. The chapel had doors that opened out into the patio. Father would be behind the altar facing us.

"On weekdays Father used to say Mass at 6:30 a.m.," José Vicencio remembers. "As you know, in

29

Cuernavaca it usually rains at night. Sometimes when we'd get up in the mornings at 5:30, and had washed, made our beds and cleaned the dormitory, it would still be raining. However, when we'd go out into the patio and Father would open the doors of the chapel ready to start Mass the rain would cease. To me this was a small daily miracle.''

FOUR

Father Wasson had been asked to form a choir with his boys so that they could sing at the church of the Third Order. Because originally it had been the chapel of the sixteenth-century Franciscan monastery, his parishioners provided the boys with robes resembling Franciscan habits.

"Singing in the choir when the church was full of people on Sunday was fine," remembers Memo, the boy who had been so happy to get a guitar. "For me it was sheer joy, loving music as I always have. It was something else to have to clean that great vault of a church when it was dark and empty. The old wood cracked. The statues of saints seemed to be souls in purgatory who threatened our somber existence, making our job doubly difficult. When we were finally finished and could at last clamber on top of one another in order to be able to reach the great iron latch and drop it into place on the ancient and creaking door, we ran for our lives and scurried up the narrow stone staircase that led to the priests' quarters."

It was while going up these stairs after Mass one Sunday morning in 1958 that, forgetting to stoop as he passed through the low arch-

way at the top of the staircase, Father Wasson gave himself a terrible blow on the head. He lost consciousness and did not regain it soon. His alarmed parents insisted on taking him home to Phoenix for medical treatment.

Padre Miguel, a young seminarian who had begun to work for Father as a volunteer assistant in 1957, recalls: "He was gone for four months. He left us no money and we had no source of income. In Cuernavaca there were sixty-nine of us boys and teachers. Every single day of those four months a stranger, a different one every day, brought us the equivalent of four dollars (fifty pesos). We teachers lived on beans and coffee so that the children might be better fed. When Father returned he asked how much money we owed and to whom. I told him we owed nothing. Divine Providence had filled our needs."

During those same four months, the first group of boys to attend high school in Mexico City were also left without funds. Their director was Al Provencio who had joined Nuestros Pequeños Hermanos as a volunteer in 1957. Provencio had met Father's brother, Barney Wasson, in the American Army during World War

II. Barney had talked so much about the work his brother was doing in Mexico that Provencio (whose home town was El Paso, Texas, where he had worked with boys' clubs before the war) accepted Barney's invitation to visit Cuernavaca as soon as they were both discharged from the army.

Barney and Provencio arrived at Nuestros Pequeños Hermanos in July of 1957. The following year, Father put Provencio in charge of the older boys who were attending the Benedictine school of the Tepeyac in Mexico City.

"In 1957, they had been there as boarders but that was too expensive; we managed to find a house for them to live in," recalls Provencio. "It was in the Colonia Lindavista, quite near the school. When we moved into it in 1958, the year Father Wasson bumped himself on the head, the windows had no glass, only one of the rooms didn't leak and we didn't have any money. But we managed — friends brought us rice and beans."

That year in spite of all the problems, the *Pequeños* at the Tepeyac school took the first ten places in their class. They ascribe it to the fact that Rodolfo González — the one from Tampico — woke them every morning at 5 to do their homework. Delighted with their report cards, Father began to dream of turning all his boys into teachers. It would be wonderful, he thought, if they who were the poorest of the poor could one day be qualified to teach in the public schools. That would be *the* way for them to render service to their own people and their own country.

Meanwhile in Cuernavaca, Padre Miguel had helped to reorganize NPH's own elementary school in accordance with all the requirements for incorporation into Mexico's System of Federal Education. The Sisters of St. Joseph of Lyon consented to take charge of this grade school.

The boys remember that the first kindergarten was located at the far end of the orchard at Buenavista. They nicknamed one of the Sisters "Madre Coquitos" (Mother Little Coconuts) because her pet form of punishing misdemeanors was by giving the boys a gentle rap on the head with her knuckles. "Come here, Pancho," she'd scold, "I'm going to give you a *coco.*"

Pancho felt tormented when school periods required him to sit still. One day, Madre Coquitos picked him out to recite the lesson. He began to recite it but did not stand up. When she asked him why he did not do so, he protested: "I can't. You are always telling me to keep still, so I tied myself to the chair!"

El Chico was another small boy who could never manage to keep clean. One Father's Day, which the boys always celebrated, El Chico decided to break his usual pattern. He washed, cleaned his teeth, brushed and plastered his hair down with pomade. To dress up to his cleanliness he found a kind of uniform among the benefactors' gifts, a splendid garment with gold braid and brass buttons.

"You will think I am a new boy," he announced as he literally leapt into the center of the patio, introducing himself into the impromptu show that the boys always set up on such occasions. "I am not a new boy," El Chico yelled in order to make himself heard over the shouts of laughter from the audience, "I am El Chico and I am going to recite for you a poem written by Guillermo Shakespeare. It goes like this:

> *Calmantis montis,*
> *Alicantis pintis,*
> *Pajaros cantantis,*
> *Elefantis volantis,*
> *De flor en flor.*

(The original version seems to have come from a doggerel verse written a couple of hundred years earlier by seminarians studying Latin in Rome.)

A mixture of Latin and Italian, one translation into English could be:

> Mountains, be calm,
> Let the spotted alligator
> And the birds sing, while
> The elephants fly from
> Flower to flower.

(Another translation: Keep your cool.)

Life at the boys' house in Buenavista was hard work. In addition to study periods and daily chores, the boys had to help with construction. The building had to be enlarged and adapted to growing and urgent needs. The first new rooms, built by the boys in 1956 at the entrance to the property, had a cardboard roof. The first dormitory looked somewhat like a chicken coop because instead of windowpanes it had chicken wire. A new dorm was needed, as were new classrooms and a larger kitchen. The number of boys was increasing but from the very moment they arrived, even the youngest of the newcomers (including 4-year-old Domitilo whom everyone pampered) had to help. The boys were going to remember the time when they worked in shifts night and day digging holes for the foundation of the new dormitory but somebody had made the wrong calculations. The holes were all wrong and they had to be filled up again. A long brick wall was built to enclose the property, but one night an earthquake shook it down. It tumbled into the ravine. The southern side of the property consisted of a steep hillside, at the bottom of which lies one of those ravines that crisscross Cuernavaca.

It was Padre Miguel's idea to level part of this hillside so as to flatten it into a sports field. It was a tremendous job but the boys tackled it with great glee. They'd have a real football field! It would be difficult to estimate how many tons of *tepetate* (that tight clay which ero-

33

sion compacts into layers in the rainy season) were carted off in wheelbarrows by the boys. Because this involved such hard physical labor, Father made an exception and paid the boys fifty centavos (slightly less than five U.S. cents) for each wheelbarrowful. "But it was such hard work," they remember, "there were usually two or three of us boys at each wheelbarrow."

A newspaperwoman who visited the house at that time reported: "The scene resembled the busy intersection of a metropolitan city with speeding wheelbarrows the chief traffic hazard. Those noisy, boy-propelled vehicles darted past each other with all the hairbreadth precision of an old-time cavalry drill."

The boys remember that in those days they seldom had enough to eat. "But we had a school," they said, "where we could learn how to overcome our own limitations so that one day we could be *somebody*."

To be "somebody" had become for them at least a possibility. Formerly they had felt like the children of "nobody" — unwanted nonentities existing on the fringes of society; but now in an atmosphere of love where they could live, grow and develop without fear, they discovered their own identities, and they could begin to hope and dream.

However, some wounds had left long-lasting scars. For instance, there was one boy who could not go to sleep if there was too much silence. Why? Had he at some time perhaps been too close to the silence of death?

Another boy could not play baseball because every time the ball was pitched to him he ducked. His father, when drunk, had thought it great sport to tie him to a tree and throw rocks at him.

When there were things like that to be forgotten, Father would tell the children that blood relationships were not important. He told them that consanguinity alone did not automatically provide the ideal characteristics of a family. Real fathers could be cruel or neglectful. Even real mothers could fail to love their children. Blood brothers were capable of hating and even killing one another.

But now here, he would go on to say, in this larger family of Nuestros Pequeños Hermanos, a much better relationship could purposefully be established. He taught the children to love themselves and each other. He demanded of the boys that they be responsible for one another *as brothers.*

He did not teach them theories. He told them to act in a positive manner, to do something nice for somebody they didn't like, for instance. He taught them to share with others whatever they had. He tried to teach them that material possessions were not important and

34

he told them never to feel sorry for themselves.

"What's the matter with poor me?" he would say in a joking tone of voice. "I am as I am. You are as you are. Both of us have to make the best of ourselves and put up with one another."

One day, a boy was brought to Father Wasson. His name was Alfredo. His appearance was ghastly. When he was 2 years old, the tenement building in which his family lived was burned to the ground. He lost everything — his home, his parents and he never knew if he had any brothers or sisters.

Someone threw him out of a window during the fire. Close to half his body was badly burned, including his face. He remembers that some women took care of him and placed him in an orphanage for eight years, where he was treated very well. It was run by some nuns, but he had to leave them because they could only care for children up to the age of 10 and he was now that age.

From there he was taken to another institution where he was miserable. The members of the staff, he felt, pushed him around as though he were a "thing." The other children either made fun of him or drew away from him in horror.

"Even I was shocked the first time I saw him," Father Wasson admits. "I wanted to help him but I knew at once that I would not be able to do so unless the boys accepted him, so I asked him to wait in my office. Then I called the boys into the patio. I told them about Alfredo and I described his appearance. If they decided to accept him, I told them, they would have to give me their solemn promise never to make fun of him nor shrink away from him — nor should they pity him, I added. They would have to decide whether they could just accept him as he was."

When he had finished speaking Father brought Alfredo into the patio. There was a long silence. The boys were very still. Then one of them stepped forward, hand outstretched.

"You are my brother," he said to the newcomer.

FIVE

The rectangle of the window had turned from grey to black. All afternoon it had comforted her to look out at the rain. It was part of the living world. The raindrops trickled down the windowpane, skidding, stopping, flowing erratically like her own blood. When the flow stopped, what would become of her children?

She looked like a broken doll, her body propped up in the hospital bed, black hair spread in a tangle on the white pillowcase. Her face was mottled and swollen, her eyes dark pools of anxiety. Would the priest never come? The nurse said she had called him because he kept an orphanage. Her hands fluttered to her throat as she felt the vague dread well up again, spreading inside of her like a shadow. Closing her eyes, she fought the pain fiercely drawing on her innermost resources. She had to stay alive until she had made provision for her children!

"Señora Arano?" his voice was soft, "Can you hear me? Are you asleep?"

"Ah no," she answered with a sigh of relief as she opened her eyes in a long pleading gaze. "Father, will you take my children? They are four, two boys and two girls. You cannot refuse!" She clutched his arm. "I am dying and they have no one."

"Their father?" he asked gently.

There was a look in her eyes compounded of despair and compassion. "He was always good to me," she said. "He can't help it; when he drinks he loses his right reason. So when I asked him to sign the paper he did. It is there on the table. Please take it. You will see that both he and I agree to give you custody of our children."

A little while later Father was standing with the nurse in the hospital waiting room, four scared little faces looking up at him. He was trying to identify them from their names on the paper. That must be Nicolás, age 12; Jorge, who was 10; Araceli, age 6; and Lulu, who looked like a chocolate doll, was 3 years old.

Helping them to carry their small bags and parcels, he tried to cover them from the night's downpour of rain as he ushered them across the street to the place where Díaz was waiting for him in the old station wagon.

Díaz leaped out to help.

"Did you bring blankets?"

"Yes, Father."

36

The four children let themselves be tucked in. They did not speak. They neither wept nor smiled. They only gazed fixedly first at one man, then at the other. The four pairs of black eyes seemed to ask the same silent question: "Can we trust you?"

Sensing this, Father Wasson said, "We will take care of you. We are taking you to your new home where you will have lots of new brothers and . . ." in mid-sentence, he stopped. He had been about to say, "new brothers and sisters." He had no accommodations for girls, no one to look after them. This was the second time that he had found himself in this same kind of fix. There had been the little girl from Tampico. He had taken her to his friend Carmen, the young mother who had lost her own daughter. That had worked out all right but here he was tonight with two little girls on his hands. What was he going to do?

Díaz stepped on the starter. Interrupting his own thought, Father made the Sign of the Cross and prayed for a safe journey.

Driving carefully along the rainy highway towards Cuernavaca Díaz was curious about what Father was going to do. He had a personal reason. He had a 1-year-old niece. The grandmother was taking care of her but the old woman was very poor and frail. Now if only Father would start a home for little girls. . . .

"Padre," Díaz ventured to ask although he knew from long experience that the priest preferred his own thoughts or prayers to talk at times like this.

"Yes?"

"Where are we going when we get to Cuernavaca?"

"A good question. But why do you ask it so soon? We are not halfway over the hills yet, or are we?"

"No, Padre."

Presently the priest said, "I have a friend; her name is Miss Julie. She is from my hometown in Arizona. She has come to Cuernavaca on a long vacation with her niece. They came to see me yesterday to tell me they had rented a house here. They said, if I should need anything they'd be very glad to help. I have the address in my pocket. When we get to Cuernavaca I will give it to you. Perhaps they will take these children in tonight. Then tomorrow we can think what to do."

The following day Miss Julie placed the two little Arano girls in a local orphanage run by nuns and offered to keep them there at her own expense. A few months later, however, to everyone's consternation, Miss Julie died of a heart attack. This again raised the question of what to do with Araceli and Lulu Arano.

It was the 1st of September, 1959. María de la Luz Blanco was sitting in Father's office typing his letters in Spanish. Ever since 1957, Miss Blanco had been doing office work for Father Wasson in the mornings and for the bishop in the afternoons. She did this work to keep herself busy. She and her mother had moved to Cuernavaca because of the mild climate. Her mother felt better in the lower altitude so they bought a house and the only thing that would have made the daughter unhappy was idleness. Miss Blanco liked to work. As she did not have to work for a living, she offered her competent services to worthy causes.

"That day in 1959," she recalls, "it was 1 o'clock when Father came into his office and suggested I accompany him to the Nolans' house for lunch. I accepted gladly. I liked them and was curious to see the guest cottages they had added to their new house which was located on the hillside in the village of Santa María, just above Cuernavaca."

At the luncheon table, the conversation turned to the problem of what to do with the Arano sisters. "I remember saying to Father," recalls Miss Blanco, "that he was always worrying about the boys but did not really care about the girls. When he began to protest, as usual, that he had nowhere to put them and no one to take charge of them, I told him that if he could find a house, I would be glad to take charge of it. At that, Mr. and Mrs. Nolan offered to lend him their own home. They would move into one of their new bungalows, they announced. Immediately the four of us wrote an agreement on a paper napkin and we signed it."

"What I had not expected," adds Miss Blanco, "was for them to move out so quickly. In less than one week I was up at their house, taking in girls, many of them babies. Carmelita for instance, was only 2 months old. Margarita (Señor Díaz's niece) had just celebrated her first birthday. In the first two weeks we took in twenty-seven *Pequeñas* (little girls), all sisters of *Pequeños* (little boys). Father sent for the sisters of the boys from Tampico.

"Of the eleven Avante children who came to us at that time from Mexico City, seven were boys and of the four girls, the youngest was 11-month-old María Ester. Her mother had died in giving birth to her. It was a terrible blow for them all. Their father was a baker, a stern, hardworking man. For almost a year he had tried to look after his children and keep his job, too. A proud man, he had been reluctant to acknowledge his inability to do both, but friends had finally convinced him to send the children to Father Wasson who accepted them on the condition that all of them come or he would take none.

It was after he had founded the home for girls that Father decided never again to separate the children of each family unit. One reason for this decision was that he had had problems with some of the boys

38

from Tampico who had been unhappy because they missed their own brothers and sisters.

"I became a *Pequeña* only because of my brother," remembers Socorro Silva. "Father refused to accept him unless I came too." Socorro (whom Father called "la Bonita" because she is so pretty) remembers that she was *Pequeña* No. 70.

It was getting very crowded at the Nolans' house and there was seldom a day without a crisis. One of the worst was the day when 8-year-old Angelica climbed to the top of a 20-foot-high wall at the back of the garden, from where she announced that she was a little yellow butterfly. Getting her down unharmed was a feat.

Then Miss Blanco became ill. The doctor said she should not be doing this type of work. After three months of it she had developed an ulcer. Father sent her back to the office where his correspondence had been piling up.

Other volunteers and later the Sisters of St. Joseph succeeded Miss Blanco as directors of the girls' home. Friends continued to arrive laden with gifts and supplies, including soap, toothbrushes, shower caps and shoes. Carmen — the one who was still taking care of the little girl from Tampico — came to help. She brought pretty dresses and shoes. She also gave the girls a weekly beauty parlor day showing them how to cut each other's hair and fix their fingernails. Most of them had arrived barefoot with their hair in tight little braids. Transformed they giggled; fascinated by their own images in the mirror, they pushed and broke it.

When asked who broke it, they replied: *"Se rompió"* (It broke itself). The bowl in the Nolans' bathroom also "broke itself." To these little girls, soap and water had always meant shivering with cold; therefore, at first they screamed their aversion when it came to having a bath or even washing their hands. However, when they discovered the supreme luxury of running hot water, many of the little ones (because they couldn't quite reach it) climbed on top of the washbowl. One day it fell apart. Jagged pieces of porcelain dropped all over the floor. Water spurted wildly from the broken pipes.

"Don't move! Don't step on anything!" shouted the volunteer on duty, starting to scoop up little girls as fast as she could and telling the older ones what to do. Rosa Avante was sent running off to find the plumber. Arcelia Estrada tried to stop the flow of water with her bare hands and cut her palms on the jagged pieces of pipe.

Virginia Nolan didn't say anything. She only lifted her eyebrows and sighed.

"What I remember best about those first days," recalls another *Pequeña,* Arcelia Estrada, "is that we felt loved. We had to work, help

39

clean the house, wash the dishes, take care of one another and scrub the floor; but to us everything was new, each day a fresh adventure. The arrival of newcomers, especially the babies, made us feel more and more like a family."

In February of 1960, the Nolans were able to move back into their home when another benefactor helped Father Wasson to obtain a large house for the girls just around the corner from the boys' house, in Cuernavaca.

Now the problem began to arise of where to send the older girls to high school. In 1960-61, Father had moved the older boys who were studying in Mexico City, from the Benedictines' to the Christian Brothers' high school and teachers' college. Neither school was coed. Nor did the houses where the boys lived in Mexico City (first in Lindavista and later in Ixtapalapa) have accommodations for girls. Father began to send the older girls to private schools run by Sisters in either Mexico City or Puebla, depending on where benefactors could be found who would take the *Pequeñas* into their homes.

He did not like to separate the children like this. Apart from the problem of distances, he feared that placing them in different cities (some of these nearly 100 miles from Cuernavaca) might make them lose the feeling that they were a family.

He decided that to emphasize and conserve this feeling, he would make it a rule that all boys and girls who finished high school must give a year of service before they continued their studies. They would come home to Cuernavaca where they could serve as counselors, help to take care of their younger brothers and sisters, do maintenance and construction, or some other work within and for the benefit of the home.

By 1963, the total number of children had increased to 396 — 300 boys and 96 girls. Of these, 60 were under the age of 6. Father felt that in Cuernavaca he did not have adequate facilities for so many little ones.

A friend offered him a building in Santa Clara, an industrial zone situated on the northern fringe of Mexico City. He accepted it thinking that even though it was surrounded by factories, the spacious locale could be adapted to the needs of the "kinders" (kindergartners). It had a big wall-enclosed yard where they could run free and at the same time be easily supervised.

Still another friend, an elderly Mexican gentleman named Don Antonio, stated his disapproval of the manner in which the children were being scattered in various places.

"Father, you cannot keep an eye on all of them," Don Antonio protested. "You are tiring yourself out, coming and going between Cuernavaca and Mexico City. Half of the time you are on the highway or in city traffic which is even more dangerous. Suppose you had an accident, God forbid; but you must think of these things. What would the children do without you? What you really need is a place big enough to put them all."

"But what about their schools?"

"You might even get somebody to put up a school on the place I have. It is the *casco* (shell) of an old hacienda which fell into ruins after the Revolution of 1910. I bought it not long after that. It was cheap but it was a foolish thing to do. I ought to have known that a dispute over the land would arise. After the Revolution, the major part of the land that had belonged to the hacienda was parceled out among the people of the neighboring villages in accordance with the law of agrarian reform, but after a time the villagers decided that they were not satisfied — even today they claim they have a legal right to some of the land that was left to the *casco*.

"I'm tired of arguing with them and I don't want to. It was never my intention to use the place as a farm. I bought it because it is one of the oldest haciendas in Mexico. It was built in the 1580s not long after the Augustinian monastery. You must not confuse the two. The monastery of San Agustín has today been converted into a museum; the other is the hacienda San Antonio de Acolman. Its main crop was always wheat, and it prospered for centuries. During the Spanish colonial era (1521-1810) some of its produce — like that of other neighboring haciendas — was used for the maintenance of the nearby convent and hospital of Tepexpan.

"It has been in my mind for some time," continued Don Antonio, "that the *casco* of the hacienda — what remains of the old buildings — could be used as a home for poor children. I will make you an offer: if you can undertake to repair the place, adapt it to your needs and run it successfully, I will give it to you."

Father Wasson said, "I am not at all sure that I could do those things."

"Would you be interested in seeing the hacienda?"

"Yes, where is it?"

"It is off the highway that leads to the pyramids of Teotihuacan. If you will be so kind as to phone my secretary what day you wish to go, I will be glad to take you or send someone to accompany you."

"I do not wish to trouble you," said Father Wasson. "If your secretary will tell us how to get there, I'm sure we can find it."

"Very well, go any time you like and I want you to do something."

"Yes?"

"Do not give me your decision quickly. At first you may reject the idea but I feel sure that if you think it over, you will see the possibilities of the place."

SIX

Acolman lies in a legendary region of Mexico. In this area, the "Man of Tepexpan" was discovered. Anthropologists say he lived 9,000 years ago and that he was a hunter of the herds of mammoth elephants which used to graze in the swamps which later became the northern shores of Lake Texcoco. When the swamps receded they left a particular type of soil that people used thousands of years later to build the pyramids of the Sun and the Moon, in Teotihuacan ("the place where men became gods").

In his history of the conquest of Mexico, Bernal Díaz del Castillo writes that on the eve of the siege of Tenochtitlan (May 13, 1521) the Spanish army led by Hernan Cortes stayed one night at Acolman and that later when the distribution was made of the estates granted by the king of Spain, the capital town of Acolman was given with its subsidiary villages and surrounding lands to one of the conquistadores, Pedro de Solís.

Although the Franciscans were the first missionaries to visit the estate of Pedro de Solís, they did not remain there. It was the Augustinian friars who built their monastery in the town of Acolman, in 1539-1560. When the friars arrived they found that the people worshiped the Aztec god of war, Huitzilopochtli. In order to bring them the "good news" of the Gospel and teach them the story of the Nativity, the Augustinian friars instituted what was to become the popular Mexican custom of the *posadas*.

These are semireligious ceremonies depicting the search by Joseph and Mary for a dwelling — or *posada* — where the Christ Child can be born. On each of the nine nights before Christmas the "Holy Pilgrims" go from house to house singing for admittance in a candle-lit procession. At the ninth house they are joyfully admitted. There are prayers and the fiesta follows.

There is a game of blind man's buff in which the *piñata* is broken. There is laughter. (If the true Mexican tradition is followed there are gifts for the guests as well as practical jokes. In the nineteenth century it was considered funny to fill the *piñata* with mice, flour or other unexpected things.)

Father Wasson was attracted by the idea that the *posadas* had originated in Acolman.

The first time he saw the hacienda San Antonio de Acolman,

however, his first impulse was to turn it down and have nothing to do with it. It was in a very bad state of disrepair. Some of the buildings were roofless and had fallen completely into ruins. Cows were wandering in and out of the main building's central patio. There were flies and mangy dogs everywhere. Upstairs some of the wooden floors were rotted. It was obvious that the plumbing had been out of order for a very long time.

That day, Father Wasson had taken two of his older boys — Rodolfo González and José Luis Ornelas — to look at the hacienda and help him evaluate its possibilities. Rodolfo and José Luis were classmates studying to be teachers. Rodolfo, who was from Tampico, was very good at counseling younger boys. José Luis Ornelas was a practical boy, a good student and one who had never been afraid of hard physical work. Both boys were good supervisors. Father Wasson felt that they were two of his very best *Pequeños*.

"I'm afraid it would cost far too much money to fix up this place, don't you think? Watch out, son," he said to Rodolfo. "Don't step there, you'll go through the floor! I wonder how much a square meter of flooring costs? Don't you think it would be better to put in tile rather than wooden floors? Of course it's in a terrible state but it would be a wonderful thing to have a farm like this where the children could learn animal husbandry," Father Wasson went on to say, as though he were talking out loud to himself. "The boys could do their year of service here."

Behind his back, Rodolfo and José Luis looked at each other horror-stricken. The same thought jumped into their minds: "Are *we* going to be stuck with the job of cleaning up this place?" It happened to them but not right away because Father hesitated for almost two years. One architect (who made no charge) drew up an appraisal. It would cost, he said, about half a million dollars to repair the buildings and more than one million dollars (the equivalent of 12.5 million pesos) to restore the whole place.

"What do you mean restore?" asked Father Wasson.

"Return it to its former grandeur."

Father studied his fingernails and said, "I think I'll send a team of my older boys, the ones who are doing their year of service, to start cleaning it up."

His friend the architect warned: "Your year of service boys won't cost you anything maybe, but don't be too sure. Once you commit yourself to take on this place, you will have the tiger by the tail."

"Father chose José Luis and me," remembers Rodolfo, "to head the clean-up team at Acolman. That year, 1963, José Luis and I were in the graduating class of the Christian Brothers Normal School in Mexico

43

City. We had to be there every day at 7 a.m. Between Acolman and this school there is a distance of twenty-eight miles. It seemed much longer. We had a station wagon but in those days there was no superhighway. The shortest route was the dirt road to Texcoco and the old paved highway from there to Mexico City.

"It was also in Texcoco that we bought all our food supplies. On that dirt road between Acolman and Texcoco there was so much dust that I had to have my tonsils out because I got a throat infection.

"To reach school on time we had to get out of bed long before dawn because we had to wake up all the boys and assign their chores for the day. When we returned at night, we would check up on what had been done."

If the ghost of some former *administrador* lurked in the dark corridor, he must have chuckled to see that customs had not changed. Even so in the old days, before the Revolution, the administrator of the hacienda had risen before dawn to assign "the order of the day" and at night each peon had had to give an account of what he had done so that the paymaster could write it all in the ledger. But now there was no paymaster with a ledger and these were not peons, nor even full-grown men. They were boys, children working for no wage at all, often shouting with laughter as they did it. They played pranks and told ghost stories to one another either repeat-ing or inventing them. There was one about the headless nun who prayed the rosary at midnight in the patio, the dead man who lurked on the stairs, the tree in the garden that allowed no one to pass it at night.

Those were figments of the imagination. The reality was that every night the boys counted their crop of dead rats. "Father Wasson had decided to pay the boys fifty centavos for every rat they caught," remembers Rodolfo. "It became a game. I had no way of knowing if a boy brought me the same rat twice. It was hard, dirty work at Acolman and dangerous, too."

The villagers were not happy to see a well-organized group on the hacienda. They tried to scare the boys away. If one or two of them wandered around the countryside they were shot at by invisible marksmen. After this had happened repeatedly Father Wasson asked the men of the villages to meet with him at the hacienda. They came.

He upbraided them for trying to frighten his children. They tried to deny this but then admitted it and insisted that one of their villages had a legitimate claim on some of the land that had been left to the *casco* of the hacienda.

"Very well," said Father. "Exactly which pieces of land are the subject of contention? My children and I," he told the villagers, "believe in sharing things. What is the earth for except that all men may share its fruits? You don't have to shoot bullets at children for this to happen." The men looked at the floor. "Now then," the priest continued, "if you will show me precisely why you feel that all or some of you have been treated unjustly, I am at your service and will gladly try to remedy the situation."

The outcome was that Father Wasson agreed it was "just" for the village of San Pedro Tepetitlan to own a particular field which had erroneously (everybody agreed) been left to the *casco* of the hacienda. At this, the men of all the surrounding villages capitulated completely and from that moment on became Father's staunch friends.

But on the hacienda a formidable amount of work remained to be done and each new task proved more expensive. When he walked around the premises listening to Rodolfo's account of what was needed Father Wasson said: "I won't be discouraged. I won't be discouraged." He repeated the words as though they were a prayer.

Only a man of faith would have expanded his activities the following year. In 1964, a high school was added to Nuestros Pequeños Hermanos' own *primaria* (elementary grades) and *normal* (junior college and teachers school) also in Cuernavaca. The project included moving the *primaria* and the younger children to Acolman.

"Father, you can't do that," his friends and helpers protested. "You don't have the money to add all those facilities to Cuernavaca. You are spending every penny on Acolman but it is not habitable yet. How do you propose to move the grade school and younger children there? Where are you going to get the teachers?"

He beamed at this last question. "We have our own teachers now," he said.

The first group of six *Pequeños* and one *Pequeña* had graduated from the *Escuela Normal "Simón Bolívar"* in 1964. Rodolfo was one of the boys and Estela, the girl. Rodolfo and Estela were in love.

Theirs was the first wedding to take place in Acolman. It was Christmas of 1964. The chapel of the hacienda had not been repaired yet so Father performed the ceremony in the central patio. The boys had hung paper streamers from the rooftops, and there was a *piñata*. It was a double fiesta, a wedding and a *posada!* Had it ever happened before? Would it happen again? Instead of marching in to the music of the Wedding March, the bride and groom were ecstatically welcomed by young voices singing:

"Entren, Santos Peregrinos, Peregrinos" (Come in, Holy Pilgrims, Pilgrims).

There was more implied than might seem by the words of the song. The newlyweds had no money for a honeymoon but they did have a home. Father Wasson had put them in charge of the house in Santa Clara, the one in the Mexico City industrial zone where the "kinders" were being housed. On their wedding night, Estela and Rodolfo went home to sixty children under the age of 6. (Later they would have five of their own.)

In 1965, the process of moving the grade school and some of its pupils from Cuernavaca to Acolman began. It had to be done piecemeal because at first on the hacienda there were only dormitories for boys. It wasn't until 1968, after American benefactors had donated a large new school building and still another with separate dormitories, that little girls were sent to Acolman.

Nevertheless, in 1966 Father Wasson appointed a girl, Socorro (whom he called La Bonita), as director of the school in Acolman. She was a *Pequeña* herself and the children loved her. "That year," she remembers, "we had 250 boys and seven teachers. The latter were also *Pequeños*. We had very little money. Fortunately, Leonardo who was still doing the work of the kitchen decided to come with us. I don't know what we would have done without him. He made both food and money stretch.

"I was not the only young woman on the hacienda; other girls were my companions. One of them was Arcelia Estrada. She and I lived in a trailer located outside the walls of the hacienda and quite some distance from the big house where the men and boys lived. One night Arcelia and I were terribly scared. We heard a tapping on the door of the trailer. It was a man. We heard his voice asking us to let him in. Arcelia clung to me and wept. I motioned to her to be still, not to answer. He tapped. Tapped. Finally he went away. The worst of it was, the door of the trailer wasn't locked. He could have walked right in.

"The next morning I told Leonardo. He sent two *Pequeños* to be our guards. It was almost worse. I couldn't sleep, thinking the boys would catch pneumonia out there in the cold night air."

Work was proceeding, however, on the construction of the girls' dormitory and the new school building. In 1967 Al Provencio was appointed general director of Acolman. Ever since 1957 when he had gone for a visit to Cuernavaca with Father's brother, Barney Wasson, Provencio has been a volunteer worker. He is still one in 1975.

It is unusual for volunteers to stay for as many years as Al Provencio and María de la Luz Blanco have done. Both Provencio and Miss Blanco — he as counselor or director, she in charge of documents and legal affairs — have given their services since 1957. It is largely due to volunteer workers that "Our Little Brothers and Sisters" has and can be administered as a home for poor children. Throughout the years

46

there have been hundreds of volunteers but never more than twenty at any one given time — most of them come and go — giving their time, knowledge and services for as long as each of them can. When they leave, others replace them. They are men and women, young and old, of various nationalities and diverse faiths.

It was a cold windy day just before Christmas of 1967 when two volunteer workers arrived in Acolman. They were the Dominican Nursing Sisters Fidelis and Philomena. They drove up that day in a trailer.

"It was the best Christmas present we could have had," reported Al Provencio. "Sister Philomena promptly won the record for flying the highest kite. Sister Fidelis could win the Olympic record for speed. In an emergency, she comes tramping up the road, her short nurse's veil flying in the breeze. Rafael Cervantes wouldn't be with us today if the Sisters hadn't been here when he got peritonitis. The doctors said if another ten minutes had passed before he was brought to them, it would have been too late.

"Sister Fidelis can place herself anywhere in the Republic of Mexico, but she learned it by getting lost on her way to doctors' or dentists' offices. She'd come back looking as though this really was the straw that broke the camel's back; but, come morning, in would come the golden chariot (the battered old station wagon) with Fidelis at the wheel, raring to go."

If these two Sisters exceed their food budget, it is a surprise to nobody. They feed Brothers, Sisters, doctors, everyone who comes to their door.

Ever since the *Pequeños* have been at Acolman it has served its purpose as a farm with livestock and crops of corn, beans and vegetables. Boys doing their year of service take charge of this type of work. Others serve their year as teachers. The older girls take care of the little children. In 1968, when the new dormitories were finished, the kindergarten was moved to Acolman.

The following is a letter from a *Pequeña* who was working on the hacienda that summer:

"Greetings from Acolman. I am settled and busy in kinder. There is never a dull moment, I assure you. I am in charge of 12 little darlings (11 boys and 1 girl). Today Paco got his head stuck in his jacket and we had to cut it off him. Tito fell down and cut his tongue. Checo sat on a pile of red ants and got terribly stung. Meanwhile Fernando and Chuco, unbeknownst to us, were in the cornfields pulling up all the young stalks. I am told this is just an ordinary day."

The children remember that one of the most exciting things that happened in Acolman took place on a summer's day, in 1971, when Al Provencio married Juanita. Juanita came to work at NPH as a volunteer in 1964. The wedding took place in the patio of the hacienda. Sisters Philomena and Fidelis were hostesses at the reception. The people of the neighboring villages brought the town band, an enormous amount of barbecued meat, huge pots of rice and beans, as well as stacks of tortillas.

48

SEVEN

In ten years the number of children grew from 72 boys in 1958 to 900 boys and girls in 1968. The constant increase in the cost of feeding, housing and educating them prompted Father Wasson to ask a group of friends — American and Mexican businessmen and women in addition to professionals in various fields as well as philanthropists — to form an advisory board in order to help him make decisions.

The first thing they told him to do was to stop taking in more children. They were not surprised, however, when he failed to take their advice. In 1970 when the number of children rose to 1,000, some of the members of this group, which meanwhile had been formally set up as an international committee, decided to change the manner of their contributions. Instead of donating diverse sums of money for the organization's general expenses, that year they made a joint capital investment which would help the *Pequeños* raise more of their own food (corn, beans, vegetables, fruit and livestock) than was already being produced at Acolman. For this purpose they purchased still another hacienda, San Salvador in Miacatlan, Morelos.

Located thirteen miles south of Cuernavaca, this 200-acre property is the *casco* or shell of what had been one of the large sugar plantations that flourished in the state of Morelos before the Revolution of 1910.

When Nuestros Pequeños Hermanos took possession of this *casco* in 1970 they found the living quarters at Miacatlan in a much better condition than those at Acolman had originally been. The reason was that although the sugar mill and distillery had been abandoned many years before and left to crumble into ruins (there were bats in the ruins and the roof of the chapel was in danger of caving in), the main building in Miacatlan was in good shape. The administrator had been living in some of the rooms. The plumbing functioned. There was electric light and a telephone. The plantation as such had not been abandoned, and most of the 200 acres of arable land are still planted with sugarcane.

A friend of the *Pequeños* who was a retired farmer volunteered to direct the work at Miacatlan for the first year or so. He began at once to plant food crops but the people of the region advised him not to eliminate sugarcane altogether because it is a commercial crop and can be sold to a nearby mill.

Father Wasson put José Díaz in charge of the boys who would be doing their year of service in Miacatlan. By this time Díaz was married and had children of his own. He was no longer Father Wasson's chauffeur but had done many different jobs at NPH over the past years. He knew nothing about farming, but was very willing to learn.

Things are always changing at NPH. For instance, the time had long ago passed when it had seemed confusing to have two Josés — two with the same Christian name. As the number of children went on increasing to more than 1,000, nobody bothered to count the number of Josés, José Luises or José Marías. In 1971-72, there were two Javiers in Miacatlan: Javier Cervantes and Javier Patiño.

Javier Cervantes stutters a little, but only when he gets nervous. He is a thoughtful boy, gentle in his movements, and slow to smile. He is more inclined to frown. "Work on the farm was not at all easy," he remembers with a frown. "The weather was terribly hot and sugarcane needs a lot of water. We had no pipelines for irrigation. We dug ditches in order to channel the water which came from a small dam that furnishes it to the surrounding villages.

"This water was supposed to be for our own personal use also, but we soon discovered that we could not use it for drinking. Several of us were knocked out by intestinal infections."

Javier Cervantes became really curious about the water which, even if boiled, continued to cause intestinal diseases. He made up his mind to study the problem. After he finished Prep, he would take the laboratory technician course at the University of Morelos. (All *Pequeños* are encouraged to continue their studies. To make it feasible NPH has an educational sponsorship program.) After he had graduated as a lab technician — Javier Cervantes went on to plan — he would study medicine, specializing in bacteriology and parasitology. Cervantes is an earnest student and inclined to be tense as well as tenacious.

Javier Patiño is a more relaxed sort of person. He is tall, eager and he smiles easily. He admits that at first he did not like Miacatlan. "But after a few days," Patiño recalls, "I got used to the hard work and to the hardships of the climate: the hot sun, mud, rain, mosquitoes and the crows. The crows seemed to think that we were serving their breakfast when we planted corn. We had to form yelling teams, shout at them as loud as we could and try to scare them off. We were perpetually hoarse.

"In the end," says Javier Patiño, "I came to like the work and I know I did it well. I helped to pick the ears of corn, take up the cucumber crop, clean the irrigation canals

50

and fertilize the soil. Above all, I liked to use the insecticide because I cannot stand for the pests to destroy the plants which, in time, bear fruit to feed my family. I plan to study agronomy. To use the land so that it will yield fruit, we have to know exactly what to do and of course we need water."

The initial lack of good drinking water at Miacatlan posed a long-term problem. Funds would have to be raised to dig a well, buy a pump, put in an irrigation system and that would all take time. For the moment, bottled water was bought for drinking and cooking as well as brushing teeth and washing. The boys went to the river to bathe, fish and cool off.

It was incredible the amount of real physical discomfort which some of the boys underwent to give their year of service. There was the boy nicknamed "Superman" who insisted on working in the fields despite the fact that he has a spinal condition and had to drag himself along the ground to help with the planting or weeding.

At the beginning of 1974 Father Wasson decided not to send the boys to work in Miacatlan but rather to have them give their year of service at Acolman. Until better facilities can be set up there, paid workers are being employed in Miacatlan. The idea of using the hacienda San Salvador for the making of food for his family is still paramount in Father's mind, however. Definite

progress has been made toward the achievement of this goal.

The well has been dug and the pump purchased, but the irrigation system still is to be built. Even with the relatively small increase in water, the commercial value of the sugar crop has taken a jump. The estimates are that it will double in the following years. Hundreds of tropical fruit trees have been planted. The yield per acre of corn, beans and vegetables is expected to multiply perhaps tenfold once all of the land under cultivation can be irrigated.

Father Wasson's plans for the future are to convert Miacatlan into a completely self-sufficient homestead operation so as to insure his family against inflationary costs. It is a long-term project which will require time and money.

Back in 1972, when Kim came to Miacatlan to do his year of service, the other boys watched over him. They would not allow him to go out in the fields alone. In the kitchen they saw to it that he did not handle a knife. They helped him cut his fingernails. They were very careful to do this in such a way that he would not feel dependent on them.

Kim was almost totally blind. He was born in the port of Veracruz. He never knew his parents. He thinks they were Japanese. As a baby he was in a government institution where a kindhearted woman found him and offered to take care of him. She managed to put him through grade school. He learned by memorizing the lessons in class. Immediately after he finished grammar school, he disappeared. After a frantic search, his "godmother" found him working as an assistant cook in a restaurant.

He wanted to be independent and a burden to no one. His "godmother" brought him to Father Wasson. His fellow-*Pequeños* pretended not to notice his physical handicap. He never felt sorry for himself because he imagined that his insufficient vision was normal.

In February of 1973 Kim was faced with the danger of total blindness. His minimal sight was deteriorating. Eye surgeons hesitated to operate. Finally one took the chance. The operation was a success. Kim could distinguish colors, his capacity to read improved and he became restive, aggressive and even insubordinate.

"Father Wasson wants us all to become teachers. I do not want to be a teacher," he protested. "I don't want to go to the university either. I want to play the guitar and study Fine Arts." His teachers and directors let him talk. They waited and finally convinced him to enter Normal School.

Then it happened again. "It was a sunlit Sunday morning last August," he says. "I was happy when suddenly it was as though a cloud had come over my good eye. I couldn't see at all! The sun of that Sunday went out for me."

In real and terrible fear Kim waited for the next inevitable operation.

Father Wasson went to the hospital the day Kim's bandage was removed. "I do believe," says Father, "it was the first time in his life he really saw me. He nearly fainted."

Recovered, Kim returned (still grumbling) to school. He fussed and fumed that he did not want to be a teacher but this last semester school was different. There were new teachers and new and challenging methods of study.

At the end of the last semester, Kim's group had to do one week of practice teaching. Six semi-urban public schools in Tepoztlan, Morelos, had been selected. This practice stressed environmental improvement.

Kim excelled at this. He helped to decorate schoolrooms, he made friends and gave lessons with great aplomb. He played the guitar and sang songs. At the end of the practice teaching, the teachers and pupils exchanged gifts. Kim had made papier-maché roosters to give to the students. Tepoztlan was filled with little children running home with a paper rooster and shouting: "Look what I got!"

On the way back to Cuernavaca that night, a thought came into Kim's mind: Christ was a teacher.

EIGHT

At the beginning of 1974, Father Wasson saw the need to reorganize the school in Cuernavaca. Because more classrooms had been needed the boys' dormitories had been moved to especially designed housing facilities that had been gradually built with funds donated by friends. The entire building at Buenavista — the one which had originally been a ranchlike house donated by a Scotsman back in 1955 — was converted into classrooms. There was a lab, and a library had been added.

Nevertheless, because of a chronic lack of sufficient funds the school never had enough teaching materials nor did it have a full-time staff. Father Wasson had become convinced that the latter was an absolute necessity no matter what the cost.

During recent years in order to get things done he had been depending more and more on his own children (he really feels that they are his sons and daughters); he had been placing them in administrative positions. A former *Pequeña* was director of the girls' home; a *Pequeño* was the head of the accounting department; another was in charge of construction and maintenance, and so on. In 1971, Father had asked Rodolfo González — the one from Tampico who had been in charge of cleaning Acolman and was now married to Estela — to return to Cuernavaca.

The Gonzálezes had left the home when Rodolfo was offered a teacher's job in the city of Jalapa. He had been getting on very well there. He and his wife had four children and another baby on the way. They came back to Cuernavaca when Father asked Rodolfo to be his administrative assistant. For Rodolfo it meant more work, a heavier load of responsibility and a lower salary; nevertheless, he gladly agreed to do whatever needed to be done. He still felt that the *Pequeños* were his brothers and sisters.

In a similar way, when it was a matter of reorganizing the school and getting a good, full-time staff, Father asked another married couple, both former *Pequeños,* for their assistance. They are Professor Ranulfo Millan and his wife, María. They had been living in Mexico City where Professor Millan had been teaching. They returned to Cuernavaca with their three children. They also brought with them a group of friends, young and enthusi-

53

astic teachers who were willing to work as a team, devoting their full time and adapting their techniques to the specific needs of the *Pequeños*.

"Nobody knows," Father Wasson told them when they first arrived, "what it has meant for these boys and girls to lift up their once broken spirits and reshape their lives. I hope you will understand and help them to develop as whole persons."

Father's problem has become increasingly that of numbers: when he had 72 or even 396 children, he could at least try to give his personal attention to each and everyone of them. No man, however, can be guide and mentor of more than 1,000 children. He has to have assistants.

The question frequently arises of what will happen when he dies or can no longer do this work. What happens when the head of any family dies or is incapacitated? What Father Wasson hopes is that his sons and daughters will be able to carry on and keep the family together.

It does have the characteristics of a family: new children arrive, they grow up, get married, leave home to take a job. Then every once in a while they come back for a visit.

It has become a tradition for NPH alumni to have an annual homecoming on the 2nd of June which is always celebrated as Father's Day. About ninety former *Pequeños* and *Pequeñas* came to the 1974 homecoming.

They all greeted one another with: "Why hello, how are you? What are you doing nowadays?"

"What are you doing with that tape recorder instead of your guitar, Memo?" someone asked. Memo is the younger of the two brothers who were brought to the home on a rainy afternoon, almost twenty years ago by Agustín, the sacristan of the Tepetates church. Memo married a *Pequeña:* her name is Magdalena. They have a little girl called Lisbeth and were expecting another baby. Memo and Magdalena were still in Cuernavaca. He was a teacher at NPH school and was trying to earn his Master's degree in Biology at the University of Morelos. Also, for several past years, Memo has been director of the *estudiantina* (Mexican folk band).

"Why aren't you directing the *estudiantina* this afternoon?" his friends wanted to know.

"Because Father decided to hire a mariachi band instead," he replied. "Somebody is writing the history of our House and asked me to interview all of you, one by one."

"Aha, ladies and gentlemen," a voice joked, "here comes the well-known reporter for Channel 2."

"I will start with you, my friend," Memo said, aiming the microphone at the person nearest him. "Will you be so kind as to tell me your name?"

"My name," the other replied, "is not really Lauro; it is José Bahena. I said so in the beginning —

don't you remember? There was already another José so I had to change my name to Lauro. I arrived at the House on the 16th of January, 1955. You and your brother Cirilo arrived the following June but it was you, not your brother, who killed all those chickens."

"*Ah caray,* that shouldn't go on tape. You mean the time we had those midnight cookouts?" Memo grinned and changed the subject. "I hear you're getting married."

"Yes, very soon. I've got a good job. I was a teacher for a while but then I got interested in electronic communications. I'm working for a bank in Mexico City." Pausing, he added, "What is your brother doing? Is he here today?"

"No, Cirilo couldn't come," Memo replied. "He, too, married a *Pequeña* and they have one daughter. Both Cirilo and his wife are teaching in a rural school located in the middle of nowhere, so to speak. It has 100 pupils and is on a ranch called 'San Felipe' in the county of Tarandacuao in the state of Guanajuato. There is no road to the school. They have to walk ten kilometers (six miles) to the place and ten kilometers back. My brother would like to get back to civilization but he and his wife realize the importance of rural schools. They are saving money and want to buy a piece of land in Cuernavaca so that later they can build their home here. The last time I saw Cirilo he told me he was trying to get the farmers in Tarandacuao to build a road so they can take their crops to market. The country around there is very fertile. It's in the *bajío* (lowlands) of the state of Guanajuato."

Lauro Bahena interrupted: "Look who's coming: two beautiful girls! Arcelia and Socorro. Are men fools that you two girls aren't married yet? You should have married those fellows in Acolman. The ones who tapped on your trailer."

"I'll tell your sweetheart on you," Socorro warned him. "Where is she? Didn't you bring her today?"

"Unfortunately, she was not able to come. What are you doing now, Socorro? Are you still with the travel agency?"

"No," she replied. "Father Wasson asked me to come back and work here at the office, in Cuernavaca."

"I'm willing to bet," said Lauro Bahena, "that you won't last long. Sooner or later the lucky man is sure to come along and marry you. And what are you doing now, Arcelia?" he asked the other girl.

"I was assistant director of the girls' house for several years, but now I'm getting a scholarship to study the Montessori method of teaching, in Washington, D.C. Isn't it wonderful? I'll be able to bring this method to our school in Acolman."

"Who else is in the United States?"

"Oh, several," replied Socorro. "One is José de Dios who is studying

55

to be a priest at a seminary in Oregon."

"He is our only seminarian, isn't he?"

"Yes, José Vicencio — the shoeshine boy from Tampico — was studying electronics in Phoenix but I hear he got married and is coming back to Mexico. Oh, have you heard that Leonardo is getting married?" exclaimed Socorro. "Of all people, Leonardo! After making the poor girl wait for more than twenty years, he is going to marry the sweetheart of his youth. Isn't that something?"

"Where is the wedding going to be? Is Father going to marry them?"

"Who else? Of course he will. The wedding will be in the little village Leonardo comes from."

"After he gets married will Leonardo go on working for us at Acolman?"

"I cannot imagine that Leonardo will ever leave us," replied Socorro. Then she turned and said, "Alfredo, how are you? We are all planning our future. What are you going to do with yours?"

Alfredo — the boy who had been so badly burned when he was 2 years old — smiled. Over the years, repeated plastic surgery had greatly improved his appearance. Strangers no longer looked quickly away when they saw his face. His friends noticed that he had beautiful eyes.

"I am studying art," he told Socorro. "I would like to become an architect but I don't know if they will accept me at the university because of this." He looked at his right arm that has no hand.

Socorro said nothing. She was wondering whether the doctors would some day find a way to attach an artificial limb. Fortunately — Socorro was thinking — he was able to do more with his left hand than most people could do with two.

"Well," he was saying, "if I can't be an architect I'll be a painter but I want to build things, design and make them. Excuse me, I want to say hello to a friend." With that Alfredo turned away from Socorro and walked up to another pretty girl.

The big hall was filled with circles of friends. The circles moved about and converged as the young men and women went on talking, raising their voices to be heard above the mariachi band.

"Of the eleven Avantes? Four of them are married and I think five are teachers."

Still other voices said:

"I have a job at Woolworth's."

"I am a private secretary."

"I am a mechanic."

"I am a lawyer, married and have three children."

"Yes, of course, some died. Of the four Arano brothers and sisters, the eldest boy, Nicolas, died. He inherited his mother's heart condition. The two girls — our first *Pequeñas* — are both married and having children."

Memo was still going around

asking people to talk into his tape recorder when a little girl ran up to him. It was his daughter. He put the recorder down on the nearest table in order to embrace her. She wanted to know what "the little box" was. He showed her, playing back the tape so she could hear the voices he had captured. Then just for fun, he taped her voice and played it back to her. Her big black eyes looked at him in wonder and complete trust. Hearing her own voice, she clapped her hands.

"That's *me!*" she exclaimed. "You put me into the little box! Play it again, play it, play it!"

Father Wasson chuckled. He had come up behind Memo and was looking over his shoulder at the little girl.

"Father," exclaimed Memo. "I didn't hear you come up. Now that you are here, let me ask *you* some questions. How does it make you feel to see so many of your children and grandchildren here today?"

"It makes me happy, but I wonder where the rest of them are. Why don't they all come back?"

"Are you proud of those who are making a success of their lives?" Memo asked.

"I don't care if they achieve material success or not," Father Wasson said. "I hope they will practice charity because that will make them lead better lives: they will love people and be of service to them."

"Father, tell us also about yourself: are you satisfied with the work you have done during the past twenty years?"

"I have not done this work alone. I have had and hope to continue to have many helpers. As for being satisfied, I never am. To me, nothing is perfect; something better can always be done. When we think we have found solutions to our problems, new problems arise that require new solutions. We think we have finished our job, but there is always another to be done."

The alumni reunion came to an end that evening but everyone said not *adiós* (good-bye) but *hasta luego* (so long). They would all meet again on the 2nd of August to celebrate the 20th anniversary of Nuestros Pequeños Hermanos.

There was very little money for this event. The festivities had to be put together *Pequeño*-fashion with ingenuity and the gifts. The banquet at the boys' house was a gift. The new drama teacher put on a very good play depicting the history of the *Pequeños,* with no costumes, scenery or props. He wrote a script but the actors, who of course were *Pequeños,* did not altogether adhere to it. The audience applauded thunderously. Father Wasson sat in the front row and wept.

A few hours earlier he had not been a concelebrant at the Thanksgiving Mass in the cathedral. He had not stood behind the altar with the bishop and other priests. He had preferred to participate in the Mass with his children; he sat in a pew with them as though he were one of them. He listened as the ancient walls of the cathedral reverberated to the sound of their voices.

The admission of new children is also held in the month of August each year. At the beginning of 1974, the usual question had come up as to whether Father Wasson should accept more children or not. He called a meeting of directors and they told him what he already knew: prices had gone up, the cost of living was soaring. The school improvements were wonderful but costly. There was never enough money to cover expenses.

Father listened and then asked questions. "Are you lacking anything?" he asked Al Provencio, the director of Acolman. "Do you have enough blankets, enough beds?"

"Yes, Father, we have enough."

"What about you, Rodolfo? Do the boys and girls' houses in Cuernavaca lack any essentials?"

"What you might call essentials," Rodolfo replied hesitantly, "no."

Father pressed him. "Would you say we have enough, Rodolfo?"

"Yes."

"Then, why can't we share what we have?" Father asked.

That stopped the argument but the decision was taken to make a thorough study of each application in order to insure that only the children in direst need be accepted. *They must have no living relatives able or willing to support them. All the orphaned children of one family must enter together.* Those are the rules but what would you do about three alarmingly undernourished children whose mother is dead, their father a drug addict? Or what about two girls aged 10 and 12, whose father and mother are alive, blind and have no income at all? Rodolfo González, who was in charge of checking the applicants' qualifications, in 1974 was free to use his own judgment.

The children are received in Cuernavaca by Father Wasson and his assistants, all of whom are *Pequeños* and *Pequeñas*. It is the latter who take in the new children, bring them food and settle them down for a little while in the classrooms of the Cuernavaca school until everybody who has registered for admittance has checked in.

Name tags have to be pinned on the smaller children who are being sent to Acolman. Off they go in the school buses. They leave early because when they get to Acolman this is what happens: hundreds of children waving multicolored paper flags are standing on each side of the hacienda's long driveway, and hundreds of voices are shouting: "Welcome to Acolman!"

The newcomers stumble off the bus with tearstained faces, some of them sick, all of them bewildered, but in less time than it takes to tell, they are engulfed by the great crowd of boys and girls who are saying, "You are my brother. You are my sister."

At first there is a tremendous amount of confusion but the children become quiet when Sisters Fidelis and Philomena start to pick out the newcomers in order to register them for medical examinations.

Acolman received approximately one-half of the 156 children who checked in at Cuernavaca on the 25th of August, 1974. However, for weeks afterwards people kept coming to Cuernavaca, bringing more children. Most of them were grade-school age. The total number of newcomers increased to more than 200.

"Stop it!" Al Provencio's voice roared over the telephone. "We haven't got room, we haven't got beds. The clinic is full." And then in a few hours his orange-colored station wagon pulled up at NPH's offices in Cuernavaca and loaded up still some more little kids.

It was in that same Fall of 1974 that Javier Cervantes — the boy who was studying to be a lab technician and later wanted to become a doctor specializing in intestinal diseases — was doing field work with his classmates from the university in a small town up in the hills. Many people were dying there of dysentery and the team of students was doing research.

Javier was startled and quite taken aback when one of his companions said to him: "You are wanted at the police station."

"I? B-b-but," Javier protested, beginning to stutter, "what have I done that the police should want me?"

"Don't worry, it's nothing bad," said his companion, "it was just that I was talking to this officer and telling him that you are one of Father Wasson's *Pequeños*. He asked me to send you to him; *he* wants to talk to you."

"Oh?" Wondering what this was about, Javier went to the police station.

The officer on duty asked if he were one of the boys from the orphanage in Cuernavaca.

"Yes," replied Javier, "I am a *Pequeño*. Is there something I can do for you, sir?"

"If you can, we would be very grateful. We have a little boy here and we don't know what to do with him. He has no one, you see. His parents were killed in an earthquake several months ago. He was sent here to his grandmother but she died. Do you think he would be accepted at your orphanage?"

"Can I see him?" Javier Cervantes asked.

"Certainly. I will bring him at once."

Javier looked and saw himself as he had been years ago: a boy alone in the world, terribly afraid, but determined not to show it, holding the chin firm, guarding the eyes.

"What is your name?" Javier asked.

The boy had a very deep voice

59

for one so small. "Isael," he replied.

To the officer, Javier said: "We would need his papers, his birth certificate and your own letter of recommendation stating that you know him to be an orphan."

"Yes, of course, anything you need."

But Javier was not listening. He was sitting back on his heels in order to make himself seem no taller than the little boy, who looked straight into his eyes.

"Do you want to come with me, Isael?"

No answer.

"I can take you to my father's house. There you will have many brothers and sisters, a great big family."

Isael thought that over. Finally he said, "Where else can I go?"

SECTION

2

THE STORY OF

"Nuestros Pequeños Hermanos"

IN PICTURES

Dawn lifts the clouds.

The church of Tepetates

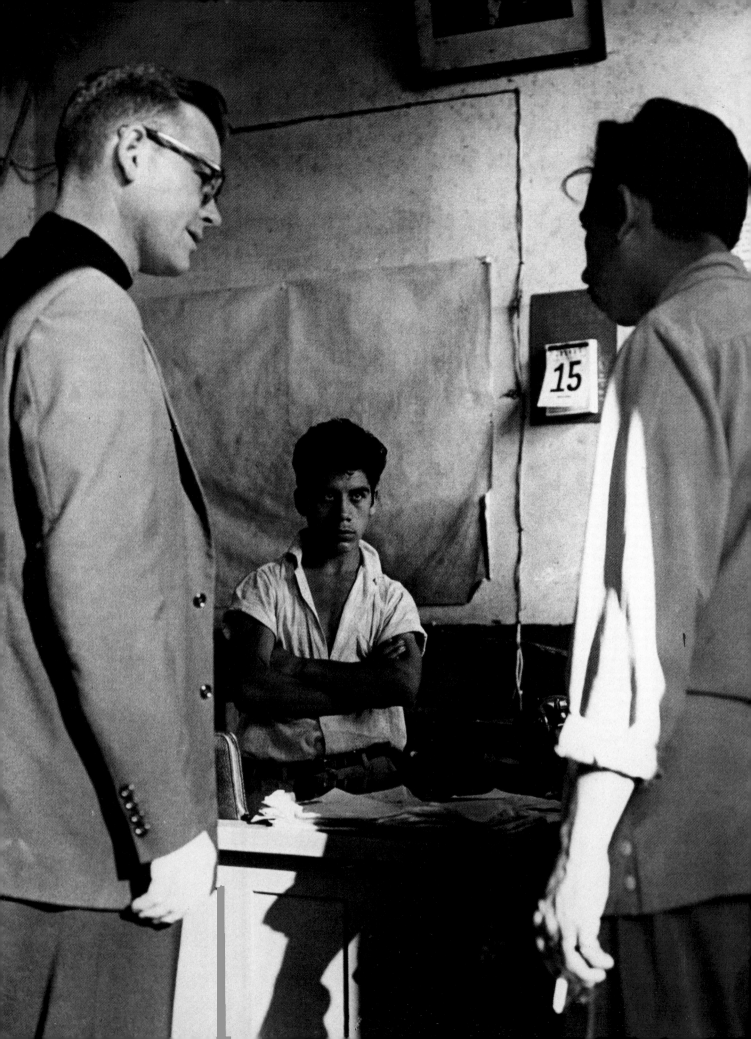

"Why, son?"

"He is our brother."

Books and goats

The dog's name was Jackson.

Leonardo

"I was in prison
and you visited me."

"I was hungry
and you gave me food."

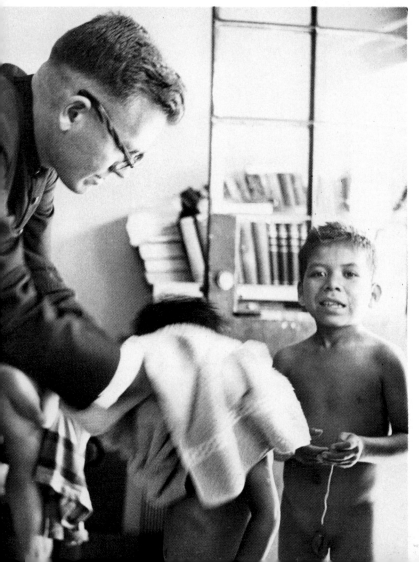

"I was naked
and you clothed me."

In flood-stricken
Tampico he looked
for the neediest
families.

The boys shared
their tortillas
with the newcomers.

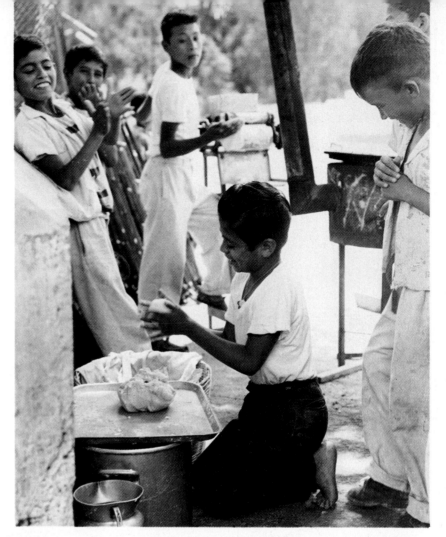

The new house in Buenavista could be expanded if the boys did the construction work and funds were available.

Miss Blanco helped in the office.

The Church of the Third Order

They had to go
to school.

The bus was a gift.

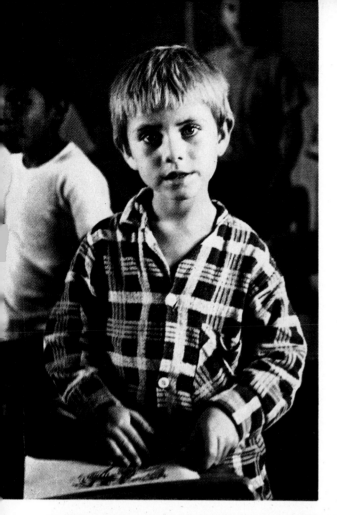

Top left: Memo and his guitar

After the death of Mrs. Arano (right) Father Wasson founded the home for Little Sisters. (Left) her sons, Nicolas and Jorge (below) with Araceli and Lulu.

(Below) Araceli years later with her children.

"I remember that we felt loved and that the arrival of each newcomer made us feel like a family."

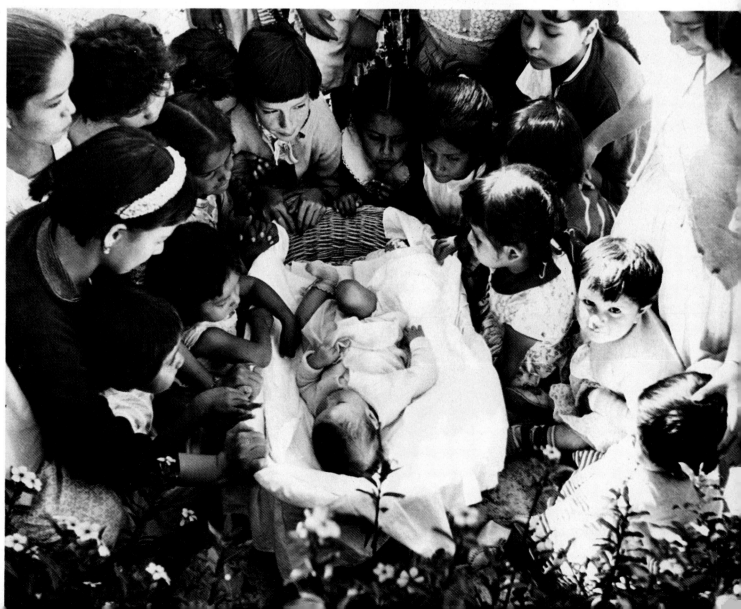

The children came from coastlines,
crowded cities and "misery belts."

The Avantes, a family of
eleven orphans — seven boys
and four girls — joined NPH
in 1959.

María Ester, the youngest

In 1959   In 1974

To take all the orphans of
one family, or none, was a
new idea: would it work?

It made them happy.

THE

The twins
David and Ramón

José Luis, the eldest brother,
became a teacher. He is married
and has a family.

RESULT

Rosa Avante married and
had a baby.

The words on the blackboard,
top right: "Have confidence . . .
I have conquered the world."

Presenting Snow White

Soda pop
on fiestas only

On Sunday

Hacienda
San Antonio
Acolman

Former granaries
in Acolman

Children in search
of a roof

Estela and Rodolfo
were in love.

The boys repaired the old buildings and friends donated a new school.

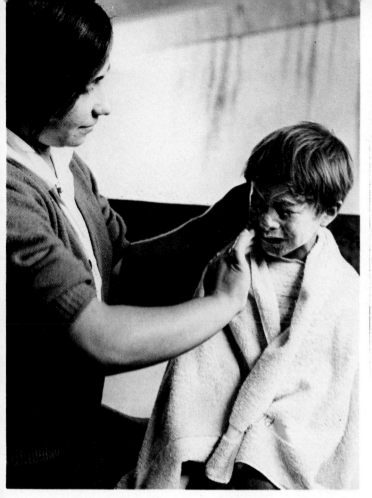

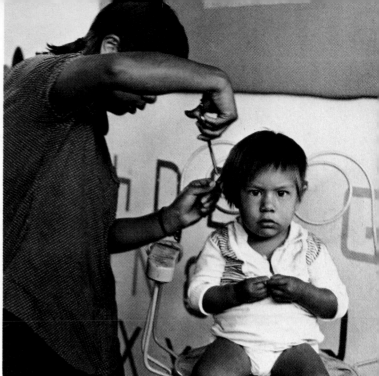

Older Pequeñas doing
their year of service
at Acolman

(Left) The new dormitory

"May your heart
open like the flowers . . ."

Kinder come to the fields of Acolman.

Happy birthday to you

S. Philomena

Nurses arrived.

S. Fidelis

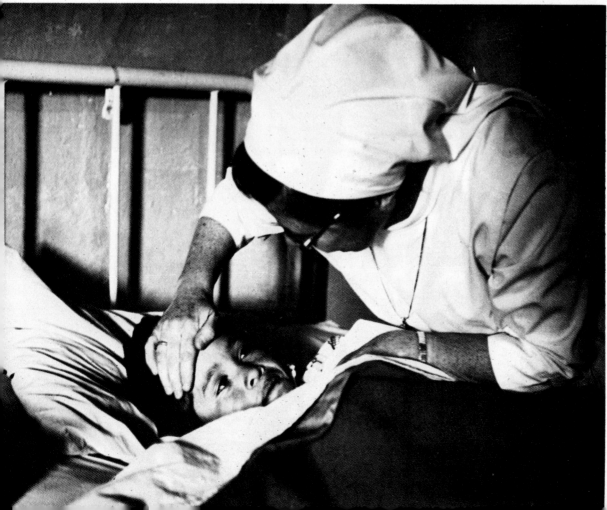

To the wedding, the neighbors
brought the band and the barbecue.

The Mexican custom
of the posadas
began in Acolman.

"In the name of heaven
I beg of you a lodging,
for my beloved wife
cannot walk."

Left: The Avante twins

"Enter holy pilgrims . . ."

"Hit it, hit it, hit it!
Don't forget to aim at it."

PIÑATA

Children come from
the hillside . . .

. . . from the tropics

. . . or from nearby villages

Their dream was a hunger for learning.

It began to come true.

Military service

Sports

Activities include
periodic visits to
museums, archaelogical
sites and other cultural
centers.

The older ones dance in Cuernavaca.

The little ones dance in Acolman.

The Day of the Three Kings

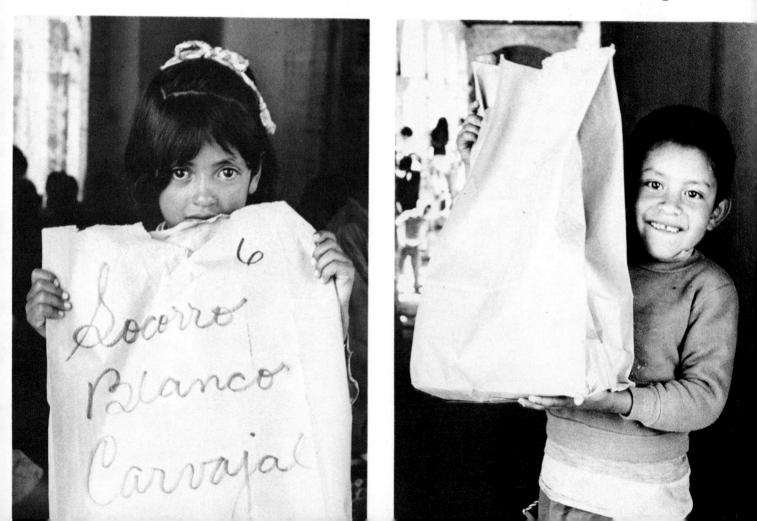

Christmas in Mexico City

The Pequeños go sightseeing.

The Zocalo

The Alameda at night

No matter what size, they all have to work.

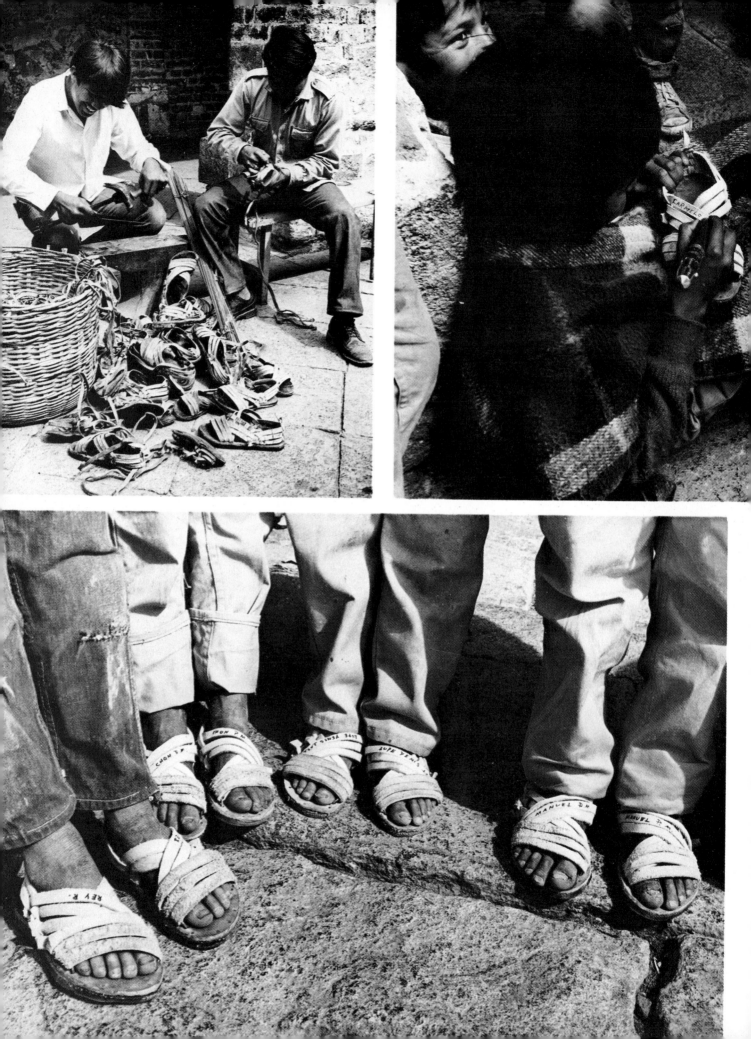

They used to make
their own huaraches.
Today they work in
the lab and the library.

As the number of children increased from
one to more than one thousand in the course
of twenty years, to provide them with a
balanced diet became very difficult. To
buy at lowest prices, the older boys shop
at the "Merced" market in Mexico City.

Even the price of cactus leaves (top left) has gone up.

Leonardo figures
each child eats
five tortillas a
day, not counting
the ones used for
making tacos.

Round rolls . . .
the specialty
of the house

"Leonardo stretched the food . . ."

. . . to fill them
again and again

. . . Teach us to share.

The answer was to raise
their own food crops.
They began to do this
in Acolman.

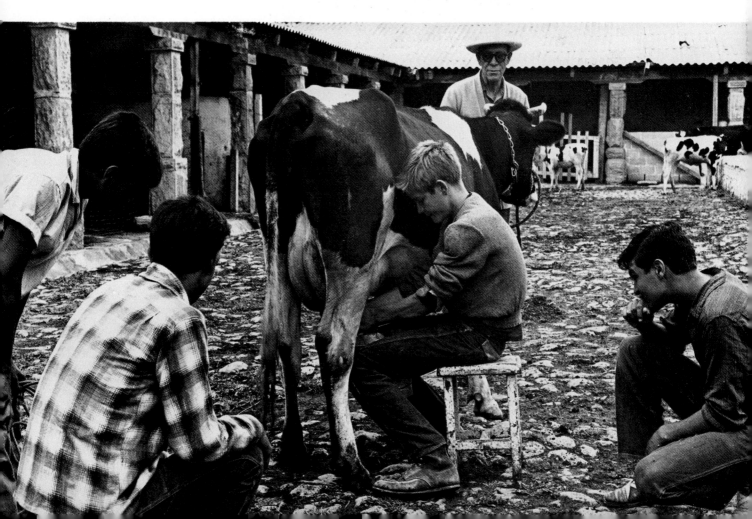

In 1971 friends donated a
second hacienda, in Miacatlan,
Morelos, so food crops could
be increased. Year-of-Service
boys worked on this farm.

Papayas and other tropical
fruit grow in abundance.

Sorghum

These boys know that to
till the land so that it
will produce the best yields
they will have to learn how to do it.

Who will see
to the children?

Don't disdain the soul
difficult to love. It is closed.
But with pain and with time
it will open slowly to hope.

Jaime Torres Bodet

The Estudiantina
folk music band
Center front: Kim

Memo and his family

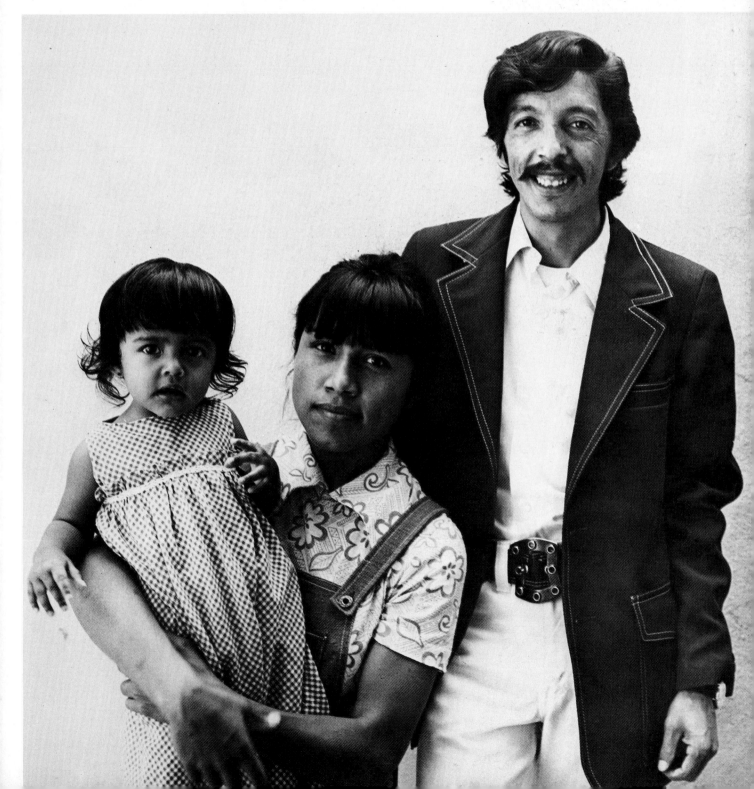

Will they be all right tomorrow?

They need
to know . . .

. . . where they
want to go.

Pequeños who are cripples
get medical attention and
they participate in all
activities. Lower right:
''Superman'' has shown his
graduation certificate to
an old friend.

Graduation

Among those graduating
in June of 1974 were
three of the Avante
brothers (center below).

" . . . and the children
asked for bread . . ."

Visitors Day
is once a year.

But few orphans have relatives.

XX ANNIVERSARY

Thanksgiving Mass in Cuernavaca cathedral

The celebrations commemorating
the 20th Anniversary of ''Our
Little Brothers and Sisters''
took place in August, 1974,
both in Cuernavaca and Acolman.

The kinder looked keyed up.

Ballet

Theatre:

Oh, happy fault

ACOLMAN

Father Wasson congratulates the actors who portrayed the history of NPH.

Rodolfo González
with his family

1974

New children admitted

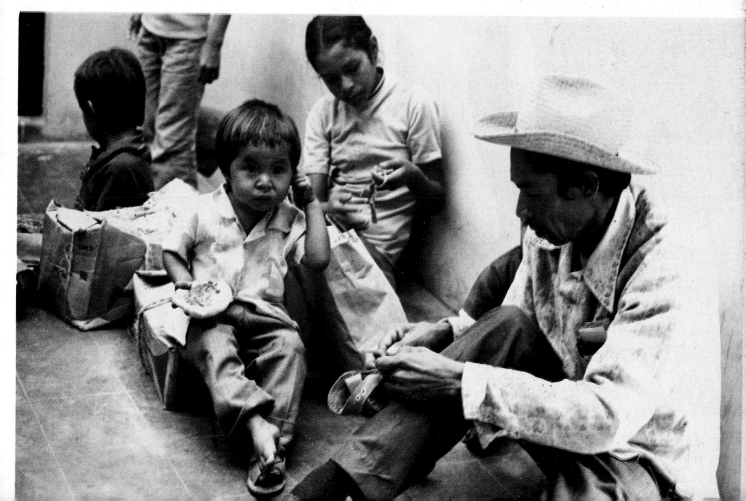

In August of each year more children
are admitted into the home of
"Our Little Brothers and Sisters."

"Why can't we share what we have?"